Tom Slemen

WICKED
LIVERPOOL

The Bluecoat Press

Contents

Introduction

Whilst reading a true crime book one pleasant sunny afternoon, a dark and curious thought arose in my mind: when did the first murder take place in Liverpool? There must have been such an event in Liverpool's misty past, when someone took the life of another person, long before the sixth commandment – 'Thou shalt not kill' – was received by Moses from God. Obviously no written records would exist of the first ever murder, as the act would have taken place way back in the Stone Age, before writing had been thought of, but it must have taken place all the same.

Since that very first 'ultimate crime', how many more people have been murdered in Liverpool throughout the Stone Age, Bronze Age and Iron Age? How many people in this region were put to death during the Roman invasion when Julius Agricola marched his forces northwards through Lancashire via Chester? And what of the fatal casualties of 1066 when William the Conqueror seized this land? The historians may argue that such killings were acts of war, but they are still strictly murders; lives were still taken. Whether a perpetrator faces his victim and plunges a dagger in his chest, or drops a blockbuster bomb from a plane and eradicates an entire street full of people, it is still murder. Also, what if an employer, through carelessness or greed, exposes his workers to daily, life-threatening situations, is he too not guilty of murder?

Another sobering thought: how many more murders will take place in Liverpool in the coming years? Violent crime is on the increase the world over, and the city of Liverpool is no exception to this unfortunate trend. Imagine how shocked a resurrected Liverpool Victorian would be if he could see his city today, in the twenty-first century. What would he make of the drug culture, for example? It is true that a few notable Victorians indulged in opium, but their children did not sell marijuana and ecstasy tablets in school playgrounds and have access to violent videos that would have horrified Edgar Allan Poe.

What would our revived ancestor make of the internet, where the most sickening and shocking forms of pornography and violence are a mere click of the mouse away? And how would the reanimated man of the nineteenth century react to the everyday sight of Merseyside Police Force's high-powered Ecureuil 'Eurocopter', racing through the urban skies as it tracks armed gangs on the move and young, thrill-seeking 'joyriders', tearing down our city streets in stolen cars? We no longer bat an eyelid to the chopper, nor to the ever-alert armed response vehicles that cruise our streets.

The omniscient closed circuit television cameras watch over us at work and at leisure, just as George Orwell claimed they would, and in the light of the ever-rising crime rate, even the civil liberty groups are accepting such 'big brother' technology to combat the criminal. Sadly, we live in a society where it is not unusual for a pensioner to be mercilessly battered to death to finance a drug habit, where children are sexually assaulted and killed on a regular basis and warped killers enjoy reduced sentences after serving time in psychiatric hospitals where drugs and pornography are sometimes available. What must be done to rid our communities of such crime? Many people believe we should bring back hanging and the debate resurfaces on a regular basis, usually after some particularly brutal crime.

In Britain, after 1945, the murder rate began to rise steadily until the 1960s, when the rate levelled off to between seven hundred and eight hundred murders per year, in a population that was then fifty-five million. During this period, it was shown that capital punishment had not deterred people from committing murders. In Britain, in 1965, the death penalty was abolished for all forms of murder, leaving treason, violent piracy, and – until 1971 – arson in royal dockyards, as the only capital crimes. In 1979 and 1983, motions for the death penalty to be reintroduced for certain murders were defeated in a free vote in the House of Commons. A politician once remarked that, depending on how you asked the question, you could expect support for hanging to run from fifty-two per cent to about ninety per cent. Ninety percent of the British public would agree to the death penalty in cases where a convicted child murderer, or rapist, kills a prison guard while escaping. On the other hand, the figure goes down to around fifty-two per cent for an unpremeditated marital disagreement which ends in murder.

One of the problems with hanging as a punishment is that, in the past, many innocent people were put to death by mistake, which is obviously totally unacceptable. Furthermore, the moral paradoxical question remains to be answered: how can we possibly kill people in order to demonstrate that killing people is wrong?

In the United States, there have been many gross miscarriages of justice where innocent people have been executed. I clearly remember a case where the Attorney General of Oregon was ordered to halt an execution because a witness had produced indisputable evidence of the condemned man's innocence – but unfortunately, the good news had been revealed just eleven seconds too late, and the process of lethal injection had already started. Horrified prison staff watched through splayed fingers as the three lethal poisons coursed through two transparent drip tubes into the arms of a sedated, yet visibly distressed, man. Could such a nightmarish scenario ever take place on our shores?

The overcrowded prisons of the United Kingdom cannot currently cope with the steady influx of offenders. In March 2001, the Chief Inspector of Prisons for England and Wales, Sir

David Ramsbotham, described conditions at Birmingham's Winson Green Gaol as some of the worst he had ever seen. Sir David claimed that conditions had deteriorated since his last highly critical report in 1998, and he accused ministers of ignoring his recommendations.

Eleven per cent of inmates claimed to have been assaulted by officers at the gaol, and one mentally-disturbed prisoner had been denied a wash or change of clothes for weeks, simply because staff had decided that he was faking his illness. Unfortunately, the deplorable regime at Birmingham's Winson Green Gaol is not an isolated case. If the British Prison Service continues to deteriorate and the costs of 'rehabilitating' offenders runs too high, other solutions will undoubtedly be sought by politicians who like to cut corners at any moral cost, in a world that worships mammon. Should a future radical government come to power, we could see a chilling reintroduction of the death penalty, possibly because it would be viewed by an ultra-capitalistic administration as firstly cost-effective, and secondly as a deterrent to violent criminals. Hopefully, such a political party will never come to power, thanks to the Universal Declaration of Human Rights, which is a pledge among the nations of the world to promote fundamental rights, such as the foundation of freedom, justice and peace. This pledge was adopted by the United Nations in 1948.

Read the macabre accounts of this book and thank your lucky stars that hanging was abolished in the 1960s, because you never know, perhaps, through an amazing set of circumstances, you may one day innocently find yourself in the wrong place at the wrong time, and suddenly become implicated in a murder inquiry!

Wickedness comes in many forms and this book is not simply a series of murder stories. In these pages you will find examples of all kinds of human wickedness, from writers of poison pen letters to wife beaters, back street abortionists, child abusers, body snatchers, adulterers, teenage gangsters, psychopaths, torturers and poisoners. You will find all the seven deadly sins here and a few more besides.

Condemned by a Twitch

Tourette's Syndrome is a rare neurological condition, characterised by recurrent tics, involuntary and purposeless muscle spasms, and vocalizations. The syndrome occurs worldwide, in all races and is usually inherited. It is three times more prevalent in males than in females. It is named after Georges Gilles de la Tourette, who first described the syndrome in 1885. It has been suggested that the English author Samuel Johnson may have suffered from a form of the disease, based on contemporary descriptions of his facial tics and of the strange vocalizations interrupting his normal speech. Another, less famous, person who suffered from Tourette's Syndrome, was a twenty-seven-year-old Liverpool sailor named William Miller, and in the year 1895, his condition ended up condemning him to death.

The events that would lead to this bizarre outcome unfolded on the Monday night of 18 February 1895, at Mann Island, an area of Liverpool's Pier Head. At this waterfront spot, which was a bustling thoroughfare back in the days when the port was a hectic hub of trade, an elderly man named Edward Moyse ran a magpie's nest of a bookstall. Moyse sold newspapers, magazines, a variety of secondhand books and a selection of Bibles.

Moyse was a church-going man, who could be seen every Sunday worshipping at St Nicholas' Church close to Pier Head, but many parishioners had their suspicions about the old news vendor. Many thought it strange that Moyse had no wife, and that he had a boy of fifteen living with him. The boy in question was John Needham, who helped his silver-haired employer during the day and lived with him at his little house at 26 Redcross Street, a mere stone's throw from the bookstall on

Mann Island. The community gossips considered this domestic set-up with the teenager to be a little unnatural.

Upon that fateful Monday, in the late afternoon, Edward Moyse left his bookstall, clutching his shabby top hat as the icy waterfront gales whistled in from the River Mersey. He was off to view a bundle of books which a man was offering at a bargain price. Meanwhile, back at the stall, John Needham was looking after the business. He sold a few magazines, several newspapers, and a musty old book or two. At six o'clock that evening, Needham pulled down the shutters at the bookshop and trudged home alone to Redcross Street.

Shortly after 6.30pm, Needham was cooking a meal for himself, when he was surprised to hear two sharp raps on the front door. Being a reclusive type, it was unusual for Moyse to have any callers, so Needham cautiously went to the door and opened it just a few inches. A dark-haired stranger stood on the doorstep. He turned out to be William Miller, a Liverpudlian sailor.

"Is Mr Moyse at home?" Miller asked, his shrewd eyes staring deep into young Needham's eyes.

"No sir, he's out – he went to look at some books to buy," replied Needham, nervously. For some reason he felt distinctly uneasy about the caller.

Without a flicker of expression on his face, Miller continued, "I was due to buy some valuable books from him, see."

"Mr Moyse won't be home until ten o'clock," Needham told him, upon which Miller returned a look of desperation.

He glanced sideways to the top of the street, then walked away muttering, "I'll call back at nine."

Later in the evening, at 8pm, Needham was making a pot of tea for himself, when there was a quick succession of knocks on the front door. The boy knew it could not be Moyse, as he always admitted himself to the house with his key, so he opened the door and found that it was the mysterious sailor who had called earlier. The man stood there shivering in the biting wintry wind, so Needham felt obliged to invite him in and told him that Mr Moyse had not yet returned.

"Would you like a cup of tea?" Needham asked Miller.

"No thank you," Miller replied, and seated himself before the glowing coal fire in the cosy living room. "If you don't mind, I'll wait until Mr Moyse arrives," he added, his voice much softer than before. He then exhibited a severe tic for the first time – the right side of his face twitched twice.

As the clock on the mantlepiece ticked on, Miller chatted about his life at sea, and the spellbound Needham was filled with glee when Miller promised: "I shall bring you home a colourful parrot and some baccy from my next voyage, lad. You can teach the bird how to talk."

Needham was warming to the sailor already and felt much more relaxed in his company than he had at first.

Miller explained that he had been one of Mr Moyse's lodgers in the past, and that he had often paid Moyse's previous chore boy several shillings to run errands. All this talk was undoubtedly Miller's method of ingratiating himself with the gullible teenager.

"He's a funny old man, Moyse is, don't you think?" Miller said, and gave a hollow laugh.

Needham gave a non-committal shrug.

"Walks all bent and hunched up he does, and likes to use long words ... " Miller started to ramble and he got up from the chair and began to pace about in front of the fire. The sailor looked around the room, his shifty eyes scanning the shelves of books and the clutter of dusty ornaments. He stopped pacing suddenly and threw a question at the boy.

"Tell me, where does the old chap keep his money?"

The abrupt, out-of-context inquiry took Needham off guard.

"Erm, I – I don't know, sir," he stammered.

"Surely you must know, lad?" Miller persisted, but Needham repeated that he had no idea where Moyse hid his takings and savings and Miller became visibly agitated. His face twitched again as he claimed that Moyse was a very wealthy man. Then, with a glint of over-inquisitiveness in his dark brown eyes, Miller sat down and leaned in close to Needham.

"It's queer that he doesn't tell you where his money is, for fear that he might die," he said.

"I don't know sir, and Mr Moyse doesn't sell enough books to be rich," the teenager informed Miller.

The seafarer patted the youth's arm reassuringly, then changed the topic of conversation.

"Well, I shall have no money worries tomorrow, because I get paid my wage," Miller said, cheerfully, leaning back in his chair, then added, "I will give Mr Moyse two sovereigns to mind. I wonder, though, if your master would be able to lend me sixpence until then?"

Before Needham could answer, Edward Moyse entered the house. The time was five minutes to ten. Upon seeing Miller, Moyse smiled broadly and the two men shook hands as the latter declared: "Oh my! I had not expected to see you again so soon."

Miller nodded knowingly, and also smiled.

"John," said Moyse to Needham, "this is the lodger I had before. He can sleep on the sofa tonight and you can make up the bed in the best bedroom for him tomorrow."

Needham was then politely encouraged by his master to retire to his bedroom beneath the eaves for the night. As the teenager lay in bed, he heard the two men in the living room below talking in hushed tones, but just what the subject of the conversation was, will never be known. Nor will the true nature of the relationship that existed between Moyse and Miller ever be established with any certainty, but Needham gained the impression that a strange closeness, which went beyond everyday cordiality, bound the two men together.

At 5am, the clock of St Nicholas' Church chimed the hour, and John Needham awoke. He yawned groggily and rose to light a candle. He hurriedly began to dress himself in the icy bedroom, when the door of his room opened slowly. Miller peeped round the door and squinted at the candlelight.

"Are you awake, boy?" he whispered, and watched Needham putting on a shoe.

"Yes sir."

"I can't wake Mr Moyse, and I can't find any coal to light the fire. Where is it kept?" Miller asked him.

"The coal is kept in a bucket outside on the landing," Needham replied, struggling to put on his other shoe.

Miller went downstairs, and before Needham could follow, the boy heard the crash of the coal bucket hitting something, followed by the sound of heavy treading. Moments later, Miller met Needham as he was leaving his bedroom. As the two met on the landing, the oddly-behaved sailor craned back his head and looked up at the ceiling.

"What's that up there?" he asked, noticing a hatch in the ceiling.

"It's a manhole, that's all," Needham told him.

"Oh, well, I must have a look up there," Miller remarked, and he went to fetch a chair that would enable him to clamber into the dusty loft.

Needham felt powerless to stop Miller and, sensing that it would be dangerous to put up any objection, he crept back into his bedroom, out of harm's way.

Miller climbed up through the hatchway, and after a noisy and fruitless search of the attic, he cursed Moyse and lowered himself back onto the landing, where he brushed himself down. Still swearing under his breath, he marched angrily into John

Needham's room, pinched the wick of the candle, and as soon as the bedroom was plunged into darkness, struck the side of the boy's head with a punch of such ferocity, that it sent the teenager flying onto his bed. By the faint light of a gas lamp shining into the room from Redcross Street, the dazed Needham saw a madman looming over him. It was William Miller, and in his hand he brandished an iron poker. He lifted it high above his head and then brought it down heavily on the poor boy's skull. Blood spurted from Needham's scalp and trickled into his eye. His legs felt numb with shock, and he was unable to rise from what seemed to be his deathbed.

"Good morning!" Miller said, and walked briskly out of the bedroom, at which point Needham passed out.

When Needham came round, he thought at first that it had all been some kind of nightmare, but then realised that his left eyelid was glued shut with congealed blood. The room seemed to be spinning round him, and now the pale light of the February morning was weakly filtering through the window. How long had he been unconscious? It was difficult to say. Needham miraculously managed to stagger to his feet and lurch unsteadily out of the room. He shouted out for his master, but no reply came.

The sight which confronted John Needham in his employer's bedroom filled him with fear and nausea and he had to steady himself against the door jamb.

The body of the old man was sprawled awkwardly across his bed, with just half of his head still intact. Above the eyebrows, the skull was smashed in like a fragile eggshell, and a 'yolk' of white and pink brain tissue had spilled over the feather-filled pillows and woollen blanket. The eyes in their bloodied sockets were turned upwards in terror towards this mess. All around the body, dark scarlet streaks and spots of blood dappled the walls and furniture.

Needham felt weak with terror, but somehow, after a few moments, he managed to compose himself and make it out into the street, where his bloodied face quickly attracted the attention of neighbours and passers-by, who immediately summoned help.

The police arrived with an ambulance, which took Needham to hospital. In number twenty-six, they discovered the body of old Moyse and quickly established that his home had been ransacked. The only money found on the premises was eight pounds, discovered under Moyse's pillow.

John Needham made a remarkably swift recovery from his dreadful injuries and recounted all the facts about Miller's visit to police detectives. Unfortunately, young Needham, not knowing Miller's name, was only able to tell the police that the man was aged about twenty-five and was dressed in a sailor's uniform. This scant description was obviously not much help in a port populated by thousands of men who also fitted the description.

"Did he have any distinguishing marks about his person, such as a tattoo?" one detective asked in desperation.

Needham struggled hard to remember.

"No sir," he said despondently.

Then he suddenly recalled something. There was one distinctive thing he remembered about Miller: the way the right side of his face twitched when he became agitated.

The detective jotted this mannerism of Miller's down in his notebook and police across the north of England were soon on the lookout for any sailor in his mid-twenties with a facial tic. A woman from the Pembroke Place area of the city heard of the killer's description and told the police that she knew of such a sailor who pulled a face when he was maddened. The police swooped on the address where the suspect was living and found a bloodstained shirt in his room. William Miller offered a lame explanation to account for the blood, saying that his shirt had become covered in blood at the Gill Street slaughterhouse, where he had held down a job for a few days.

Police took Miller to the abattoir and asked him to pinpoint the exact spot where he had been working when he had killed the animals.

"I was working just here. I remember one animal giving me a lot of difficulty and it struggled as it bled all over me," Miller elaborated.

After his detailed description of his work at the slaughterhouse, the abattoir superintendent told the police and Miller that they had not killed any cattle in that part of the building for almost five months.

"Those carcasses you see over there were brought over from Birkenhead to be sold here," he added.

Miller seemed to choke as he attempted to respond, his throat no doubt bone dry because he realised that his alibi had been blown apart. Police escorted the murderer to the bedside of John Needham, who was still being treated in hospital for the severe injuries to his skull. Needham was not absolutely sure if Miller was the man who had visited the house in Redcross Street, as the blows to his head had scrambled his memory somewhat. A line of men was assembled at the end of the boy's bed, and Needham studied each of their expressionless faces in turn. One face looked very familiar, and that was the face of William Miller, the man who was standing second to last in the line-up. Needham knew that if he was mistaken, the killer of old Mr Moyse would walk the streets a free man – and what if he came back to kill off the only witness to the murder?

Needham again studied the gallery of blank faces before him. The men in the identity parade stared straight ahead at the wall above Needham's bed – except for one. His dark eyes burned into the boy's anxious eyes. That look said it all. Those brown eyes despised Needham and the evil mind behind them probably regretted not having finished off the teenager when he had the chance.

Then came the ultimate confirmation of Needham's grave suspicion: the stress of the situation had caused the right side of the man's face to start twitching uncontrollably. There could be no doubting it now; he was definitely him the man who had attacked him.

Needham shuddered with fear but bravely pointed his finger at Miller.

"Look! Look at his face! That's him!" he cried. "He killed Mr Moyse! That's him!"

The boy suddenly crumpled and started to cry. As three policemen grabbed hold of Miller and dragged him out of the hospital room, the poor lad took refuge under the blankets.

William Miller was subsequently tried for the murder of Edward Moyse and the attempted murder of his assistant, John Needham, and he was then hanged at Walton Gaol.

Unrequited Love

Early in the last century, at 46 Upper Parliament Street, there stood a fine new church called the Temple of Humanity. The religion, or rather, the philosophy, of those who attended the temple was known as 'Positivism', a belief-system that was founded by the French philosopher and sociologist, Auguste Comte. Positivists do not worship God as such, but are, instead, devoted to humanity, and they strive to improve the welfare of the human race as a whole.

If you were to stroll along Upper Parliament Street today, with the Anglican Cathedral and the end of Hope Street to your left, you would come upon a red brick church with a curious architectural feature. High up the front central wall of the church, there is a curiously vacant arched recess. This dark and empty arched vault once housed a poignant statue of a mother and child. The reasons behind the removal of the statue? – a double murder, an attempted murder, and a suicide, that took place one autumnal evening in 1913. Let us first go back further in time, just a few years before the murders, to uncover the seeds of the sensational killings.

The leader of the Positivists in Liverpool was Sydney Styles, a solicitor who lived with his wife at 69 Hope Street. At this address, each Thursday evening, the Positivists held soirées and received new members. One new member who was introduced to the sect was a handsome Evertonian carpenter, named William MacDonald. MacDonald was presented to the Positivists by a rather naive copper engraver named Richard Price Roberts, who admired the carpenter's Marxist leanings.

MacDonald was soon accepted into the sect and found that their creed was very similar to the ideals of the Communist manifesto. He spent many an hour at the Hope Street address each Thursday, passionately discussing his views on Socialism and extolling dialectical materialism.

Alas, MacDonald had another passion, but it was one he never dared to express or admit to. This other passion was his secret love for Mary Crompton, the forty-two-year-old daughter of Albert Crompton, a prominent shipping magnate and co-founder of the Positivists. Mary was also the grand-daughter of Sir Charles Crompton, who was a Justice of the Queen's Bench.

All contemporary accounts agree that Mary was beautiful, and unintentionally sensual. She had strawberry blonde hair, china blue eyes, a childlike face and a curvaceous figure. Although she was from the upper reaches of society, she never distanced herself from her lower class roots and always found time to help the down-trodden and disadvantaged. She was also highly educated, well-read and fluent in many languages. However, since she had so many virtues and accomplishments, many people wondered why she had never married. There were whispered tales of a man who had broken off his engagement to Mary, twenty years before, and that she had never recovered from the heart-breaking experience.

Mary certainly had no shortage of admirers. One young man, Paul Gaze, was infatuated with her, despite an age difference of eighteen years. He was an orphan who had been adopted by Miss Compton. Many times during his teens and early adulthood, Paul had confronted his patroness on bended knee, declaring his love for her, and each time Mary had told him that the nature of the love that burned in her breast for him could only be platonic and maternal. Paul had spent many tearful nights sobbing in Mary's arms, as a result of his inability to accept what he interpreted as her rejection of him.

Fortunately, Paul eventually found employment with a chemical-manufacturing firm, and during an overseas stint as a representative of this firm, he met a beautiful Brazilian girl. He fell deeply in love with her and they were engaged to be married. When he brought his fiancée home with him, he announced his plans to marry her to the Positivists, which brought a tear to Mary Crompton's eye. Mary was relieved that Paul had at last found someone nearer to his own age-group, yet she also found herself envying him. Perhaps she was envisaging the happily married life she had longed for over the past twenty years.

After Paul Gaze had married, Mary Compton remained a good friend and a virtual mother to the couple, but the green-eyed monster in William MacDonald viewed the relationship cynically. MacDonald imagined that his secret love was becoming increasingly fond of Paul Gaze, and he could not allow that. All his Marxist ideals of common ownership were applicable to the materialistic world, but as far as Miss Crompton's benevolence and love was concerned – that should be reserved for him alone. His jealousy burned painfully within his soul, like a slow fuse, consuming all reason.

Matters finally came to a head one night at 9.30pm, on Tuesday, 7 October 1913. The emotionally-torn MacDonald armed himself with a revolver and a weighted stick, and he set off to the house of Richard Price Roberts, the copper engraver who had introduced him to the Temple of Humanity. As far as the demented MacDonald was concerned, Roberts was yet another rival, who had been getting a bit too familiar with Miss Compton of late. Now it was time to remove him from the arena.

MacDonald rang the bell of Roberts' house and waited. A few moments later there were footsteps in the hall and the door opened wide. Roberts stepped out and smiled innocently, about to greet his friend. Without speaking, MacDonald brought the heavy stick down on Roberts' head. The copper engraver's legs buckled and he started to slide down the doorframe with a puzzled expression etched on his face. The carpenter then drew a revolver and aimed it point blank at Roberts' head. The engraver was too terrified to make a move, but simply closed his eyes, awaiting the end. MacDonald fired twice. One bullet missed, by a fraction of an inch, but the second one passed straight through Roberts' nose, spraying the hallway walls with a sickening mess of cartilage and blood. The bullet had passed through the victim's nose and embedded itself in the vestibule door. Roberts slumped onto the floor, bleeding profusely in an unconscious state. Amazingly, he later recovered from the shooting and bludgeoning which he had received at the hands of his one-time friend.

Ten minutes later, MacDonald was dashing through the night to 26 Grove Street, less than a quarter of a mile from the scene of the attempted murder. His next victim was another imagined arch-rival in love, the newly-married Paul Gaze. When MacDonald called at his home, the young man cheerfully invited him in. About twenty minutes later, at 10.15pm, the maidservant at the Gaze residence heard two loud noises, which sounded like a cane being rapped on a door.

What she had actually heard was the sound of two gunshots. When the maid set off to investigate the origins of the loud reports, she heard running footsteps in the hall. She then noticed that the front door of the house was wide open. With a rising sense of panic, she closed the door and entered the parlour to find Paul Gaze lying dead on the hearth rug. There was a bullet wound in his temple and the wall near the fireplace was speckled with crimson blood and white scraps of brain matter. The exit wound in Paul's head was a gaping hole, five inches in diameter.

MacDonald, meanwhile, had discarded the stick, and was once again charging through the night in a frenzy to kill another victim. He ran down Myrtle Street on that freezing moonlit night and turned left into Bedford Street South. By now he had tears in his eyes, as he wallowed in self-pity. He arrived at number 81 and hammered on the door knocker. The woman he idolised lived here – Miss Mary Crompton – his next victim. MacDonald wiped his tears on his cuffs.

A maid answered the door and MacDonald lunged towards her and asked for Miss Crompton with a tone of desperation in his voice.

"Miss Crompton has just retired to her room," the maid told him, in some alarm.

"Please, I have to see her now," MacDonald insisted, "it is of the utmost urgency!"

The maid invited MacDonald into the sitting room and hurried off to fetch Mary. Minutes later, Mary Crompton, the innocent victim of her own charisma, came downstairs to meet MacDonald.

"Yes William?" she asked, gently, perhaps wondering if the carpenter had come to deliver some tragic news which could not wait until the morning.

William MacDonald was face to face with the object of his unrequited love. It is said that unrequited love is the cruellest love of all, and the only love that lasts forever, but this meeting between William and Mary was to be the final act in a romantic tragedy.

"I loved you," William MacDonald whispered to Mary in a quaking, broken voice, and then he quickly produced the revolver and, in one swift movement, he placed its barrel against Mary's beautiful forehead.

"Oh!" Mary uttered as she finally realised his intent, and the maid screamed in the hallway.

Mary Crompton died instantly. She fell to her knees first and glanced up at William MacDonald with a half smile as blood flowed copiously down one side of her face. She then fell forward and her head landed at his feet.

The maid watched in horror as MacDonald turned the gun on himself. He pressed the mouth of the barrel to the side of his temple and looked at the maidservant with an expression of pure emptiness. He pulled the trigger, and blew part of his brains out. He fell beside Mary, but he did not die immediately. He gazed at the ceiling, wide-eyed, and his entire body trembled as he foamed at the mouth. He whispered the name 'Mary' repeatedly, before lapsing into a comatose state. He died from his self-inflicted injuries three hours later, at the Royal Infirmary.

After the double murder, suicide and attempted murder, the Positivists decided to disband; the shame associated with member, William MacDonald, never went away. By 1947, the number of members attending the Temple of Humanity had dwindled to such an extent, that it was decided that the statue which had been representative of the sect – a mother holding a child – should be taken down from its arched recess. The Positivists had been virtually destroyed by one of the most powerful emotions known to humanity – jealousy.

The Half-Hanging of James O'Connor

On the evening of 11 August 1873, a 29-year-old Liverpool boxer named James O'Connor, left Cambridge Music Hall in Mill Street, Toxteth. The concert had ended and as the audience spilled out onto the street, O'Connor noticed an attractive-looking woman who had emerged from the hall and, for some reason, he took her to be a prostitute. However, the woman was not a harlot, but a respectable married lady, and when O'Connor asked her to accompany him to a local public house to have a drink and an intimate chat, the woman politely but firmly rejected the man's advances and walked on into the night.

O'Connor would not, or could not, take no for an answer and he stalked her for quite some distance. When the woman became aware of him following her, she turned around and angrily told him to leave her alone. At this, O'Connor suddenly accused her of being a whore who had accepted his money, but had not provided her services yet. The woman turned red with embarrassment at this unfounded accusation, in such a public place, and started to quarrel with O'Connor. The argument became so heated that the woman screamed an insult at O'Connor and he reacted by striking her across the face twice. Being a boxer, his blows sent her hurtling across the pavement. She landed on her back with a sickening thump and appeared to be semi-conscious.

The cowardly assault was witnessed by two passers-by on the other side of the street, and one of them, a man named Jim Gaffney, ran across the road and confronted O'Connor.

"What did you do that for?" Gaffney asked, looking down at the woman lying moaning on the pavement.

O'Connor offered no reply, but instead reached into the inside pocket of his jacket and produced a clasp knife. Without further warning, he plunged the blade of this knife deep into Gaffney's neck.

Having witnessed this horrific incident, Gaffney's friend, a man named Metcalf, hurried over the road and delivered a straight punch to O'Connor's jaw, which sent the boxer reeling to the ground. However, being a deft practitioner of the noble art of pugilism, O'Connor was quick to recover from the blow, and, pulling himself to his feet, he rammed the knife into Metcalf's torso. O'Connor then sped off into the twilight, as his innocent victims lay bleeding on the pavement, in a critical state.

Gaffney and Metcalf were soon taken to the Southern Hospital. Metcalf subsequently made a complete recovery, but Gaffney started to choke on his own blood, as the internal bleeding from the artery in his neck could not be stopped, no matter how hard the surgeon tried to stem the flow. On the following morning, the gallant good Samaritan died.

After taking statements from Metcalf and the woman who had innocently been at the centre of the dreadful events which had led to the killing, the police were swift in tracking down O'Connor, who was a well-known troublemaker, with a fondness for using blades. He was arrested and charged with Gaffney's murder together with the attempted murder of his friend, Metcalf.

Before Judge Brett at the following Assizes at St George's Hall, O'Connor was found guilty of the murder of James Gaffney and the attempted murder of Metcalf. He was sentenced to hang at

Kirkdale Gaol early in September. When the execution date arrived, O'Connor could not have imagined the cruel, traumatic debacle he would have to endure before the rope finally snapped his neck. In the weeks before the execution, he had probably gone over the forthcoming events many times in his mind, envisaging a swift death at the end of the rope and taking some small consolation from the thought.

On the Monday morning of the execution, at eight o'clock precisely, the public executioner, an allegedly experienced man by the name of Calcraft, escorted O'Connor, who was accompanied by a priest, Father Bronte, onto the scaffold, in the corner of the prison yard. Calcraft had hanged hundreds of people during his career, and had supervised many mass-hangings at Tyburn, so Father Bronte probably assumed that the executioner knew his job well enough to end O'Connor's life with the minimum of distress.

Calcraft carefully positioned O'Connor over the trap-doors. The condemned man stood there shivering with apprehension, putting on what was a blatantly false smile for the benefit of the six newspaper reporters who stood nearby, waiting to observe the gruesome proceedings. The white cap was about to be placed over O'Connor's head, when Father Bronte stepped forward and offered the condemned man a crucifix to kiss. O'Connor trembled and kissed the crucifix with seeming reverence. By now, James O'Connor was shaking violently and blinking repeatedly. The white cap was pulled over his face and Calcraft placed the noose around his neck and drew it tight. O'Connor muttered something unintelligible as Calcraft bound his wrists and then his legs together with thick leather straps. Father Bronte started to recite a prayer, and there was a startling crash as Calcraft drew the bolt.

O'Connor plunged to what should have been a sure and instantaneous death – but the rope had snapped! He wriggled about in the pit below the scaffold, screaming in agony. Bound, and unable to see a thing because of the hood that covered his head, O'Connor was confused and distressed, to say the least. Horrified, Father Bronte jumped down into the pit with one of the pressmen. The cleric pulled back the hood from O'Connor's head and tried to console him as he loosened the noose from his rope-burned neck.

O'Connor ignored the priest and turned to the newspaper reporter with tears welling up in his eyes.

"I stood it bravely, didn't I? You'll let me off now, won't you?" he pleaded.

The reporter made no answer, but scribbled O'Connor's desperate words into his notebook.

"What do you call this?" O'Connor screamed hysterically, sensing that perhaps he would not be let off after all. "Do you call this murder?" he went on, and broke down, sobbing.

As Calcraft went in search of another rope, Father Bronte tried to draw O'Connor's attention to an extract from the *Book of Devotions*, but the half-hanged man screamed inconsolably.

"I have not got over the pain! Lord have mercy on me!" he cried.

The pressman continued to record O'Connor's words and left the pit in the certain knowledge that he would soon make a second drop, because the law was specific and absolute on the matter: 'There to be hanged by the neck until you are dead'. And the law was to be obeyed.

Within minutes, James O'Connor found himself standing once again on the awful trap-doors, with a noose of new, reliable rope about his neck. By now the condemned man had adopted such a defeatist attitude, that Calcraft allowed him to adjust the noose himself and pull the white cap over his own face. Moments before the bolt was drawn, he stood there silently, with his head bowed. When he fell for the second time, he took a full eight minutes to die, because this time, Calcraft had made a gross error in calculating the length of the rope. Probably, in the confusion following the first bungled attempt, he had only allowed for a drop of eight inches, and because of this second, serious blunder, the hangman was never asked to despatch anybody again at Kirkdale Gaol.

Human Guinea Pigs

In 1865, there was an outbreak of smallpox in Liverpool. Vaccination in those times was primitive and often produced horrific and usually fatal side effects, as the following medical report of the Royal Commission details. It is the evidence of a Dr Thomas Skinner of Liverpool.

'A young lady, fifteen years of age, living at Grove Park, Liverpool, was re-vaccinated by me, at her father's request, during an outbreak of smallpox in Liverpool in 1865, as I had re-vaccinated all the girls in the Orphan Girls' Asylum, in Myrtle Street, Liverpool (over two hundred girls, I believe), and as the young lady's father was chaplain to the asylum, he selected, and I approved of the selection, of a young girl, the picture of health, and whose vaccine vesicle (a pimple-like sac of fluid on the skin) was matured, and as perfect in appearance as it is possible to conceive.

On the eighth day, I took off the lymph in a capillary glass tube, almost filling the tube with clear, transparent lymph. Next day, 7th March, 1865, I re-vaccinated the young lady from this same tube, and also from the same tube and at the same time, I re-vaccinated her mother and the cook. Before opening the tube I remember holding it up to the light and requesting the mother to observe how perfectly clear and homogeneous, like water, the lymph was, neither pus nor blood corpuscles were visible to the naked eye.

All three operations were successful, and on the eighth day all three vesicles were matured, "like a pearl upon a rose petal", as Jenner described a perfect specimen. On that day, the eighth day after the operation, I visited my patient, and to all appearance she was in the soundest health and spirits, with her usual bright eyes and ruddy cheeks. Although I was much tempted to take the lymph from so healthy a vesicle and subject, I did not do so, as I have frequently seen erysipelas and other bad consequences follow the opening of a matured vesicle. As I did not open the vesicle, that operation could not be the cause of what followed.

Between the tenth and the eleventh day, after the re-vaccination, that is, about three days after the vesicle had matured and begun to scab over, I was called in haste to my patient, the young lady, whom I found, in one of the most severe rigors I ever witnessed, such as generally precedes, or ushers in, surgical, puerperal, and other forms of fever. This would be on the 18th March, 1865.

Eight days from the time of this rigor, my patient was dead, and she died of the most frightful form of blood poisoning that I ever witnessed, and I have been forty-five years in the active practice of my profession. After the rigor, a low form of acute peritonitis set in, with incessant violent vomiting and pain, which defied all means to allay. The young lady screamed for mercy and her eyes rolled about. At last, stercoraceous vomiting and cold, clammy, deadly sweats of a sickly odour set in, with pulselessness, collapse, and death, which closed the terrible scene on the morning of the 26th March, 1865.

Within twenty minutes of death, rapid decomposition set in, and within two hours, so great was the bloated and discoloured condition of the whole body, more especially of the head and face, that there was not a feature of this once lovely girl recognisable. The pressure from within the corpse was so intense, pus and clear liquid squirted forth from the tear ducts and nostrils. Dr John Cameron, of 4 Rodney Street, Liverpool, physician to the Royal Southern Hospital at Liverpool, met me daily in consultation while life lasted. I have a copy of the certificate of death here.

I can attribute the death there to nothing but vaccination.'

In the same report, fifteen medical men gave evidence as to disease, permanent injury, or death, caused by vaccination. Two gave evidence of syphilis and one of leprosy as clearly due to vaccination. As an instance of how the law regarding medical blunders is applied to the poor, we have the story told by Mrs Amelia Whiting.

In brief, it amounts to this; Mrs Whiting lost a child, after terrible suffering, from inflammation supervening upon vaccination. The doctor's bill for the illness was one pound, twelve shillings and sixpence and a woman who came in to help was paid six shillings. After this first child's death, proceedings were taken for the non-vaccination of another child; and though the case was explained in court, a fine of one shilling was inflicted. The husband's earnings as a labourer were eleven shillings a week.

Murder on the High Seas

In April 1857, a gentle but retarded seaman named Andrew Rose joined the crew of the barque *Martha and Jane*, which was anchored off Barbados. It did not take Captain Henry Rogers long to discover that the new member of his crew possessed a slow-witted mind, and Rogers and his despicable cronies – William Miles (first mate) and Charles Seymour (second mate) soon began to make Rose's life a misery.

Seymour gave Rose a simple task to perform on the ship, but was not satisfied with the way in which the newly-recruited mariner set about his job, so he punched and kicked him until he was black and blue. After the savage and gratuitous beating, several members of the crew took pity on Rose and urged him to run away. Rose took their advice and fled the ship, but shortly afterwards he was captured by the police and taken back to the *Martha and Jane*, where he was put in irons.

Now Rogers had a genuine excuse to unleash his brutal nature, and shortly after the barque set sail for Liverpool, Rose was mercilessly thrashed by the captain and the first and second mates. They kicked him and then whipped him with a length of rope until they were exhausted, leaving the unfortunate half-wit's body a blood-soaked mess.

The cruelty did not stop there. Days later, the shackled Rose somehow mustered the inspiration to sing a hymn. His singing immediately summoned Captain Rogers onto the deck. Rogers instructed the first mate to fetch him a large iron bolt, which he proceeded to ram into Rose's mouth. Miles and Seymour made sure that the bolt, which was threatening to choke Rose, was kept securely in place by tying a strong length of yarn around Rose's head. The sadistic captain and his henchmen forced Rose to endure this ordeal for an hour-and-a-half, before finally removing the bolt.

Another of the captain's perverted little pleasures was to set his dog onto Rose with the command, "Bite that man!" The dog would charge at the unfortunate mariner and actually bite off chunks of his flesh. Many of the bite wounds sustained by Rose in this way later became badly infected and oozed with pus. Rose's appalling state of health did not prevent the captain from sending him naked up the mast, to furl the sail, with the first mate following behind with a whip. The ultimate humiliation which the sadistic Captain Rogers imposed upon the poor man, was to make him eat his own excrement.

When the ship was a week out from Liverpool, Captain Rogers was standing on deck, surveying the pathetic, sore-covered body of Andrew Rose, with an expression of contempt etched on his cruel, weather-beaten face, when he suddenly remarked, "Rose, I wish you would either drown, or hang yourself".

Rose had endured enough, and did not care any more; he wanted to be rid of his terrible suffering, and he replied, "I wish you would do it for me".

Rogers reacted venomously to this mildly audacious hint of insubordination; he and the two mates grabbed Rose by the arms and dragged him to the mainmast. A rope was produced and a noose was quickly made. They put the noose over Rose's head and hanged him from the mainmast for two full minutes. At the end of this time, Rose's eyes were bulging, and his protruding tongue was starting to turn black. The captain gave the order to release him, and Rose dropped to the deck with a thump and lay there, inert. He was barely alive.

Without a trace of compassion or feeling in his voice, Captain Rogers boasted to his crew, "If I'd kept him there just half a minute longer, he'd have been a goner!"

However, the terrifying treatments proved too much for Andrew Rose, and shortly afterwards, on 5 June 1857, after staggering onto the deck in a semi-conscious state, the mentally disadvantaged mariner weakly cried out, "Why?" and then dropped down dead.

The crew found the sight and stench of Rose's ulcerated and maggot-infested body unbearable and complained to the captain, who ordered his men to throw the festering corpse overboard into the sea.

Four days later, the *Martha and Jane* docked at Liverpool, and several members of the crew, sickened by the events they had witnessed, immediately reported Captain Rogers and the mates to the authorities. Rogers and his two partners in crime were taken into custody, and at St George's Hall, on 19 August, they were tried for the murder of Andrew Rose. The jury found them guilty, and when word of the verdict reached the huge mob assembled outside the building, Lime Street echoed to the sound of jubilant cheering.

The hitherto callously brutal personality of Captain Rogers apparently underwent a dramatic change while he awaited execution in his cell at Kirkdale Gaol. He turned to God and prayed almost constantly throughout his final lonely days and nights.

On 12 September at noon, the captain, who had taken sadistic delight in torturing a simple-minded man and robbing him of his life, sampled some of the fear that Andrew Rose had felt under his wicked hand, when he was taken to the scaffold, in full view of a crowd of thirty thousand laughing and jeering spectators. Until the white cap was pulled over his face by the hangman, Rogers stood on the gallows, erected near the top of the prison wall, and stared out at the sea's horizon, beyond the crowds below, beyond Liverpool Bay. The eternal sea was the last thing on earth which the captain saw; the sea that had been his life – and Andrew Rose's premature watery grave.

After the hanging, a subscription was opened for the widow and five children of Captain Rogers, and six hundred and seventy pounds was collected, quite a substantial sum in those days.

The Leveson Street Massacre

Mrs Ann Hinrichson, a twenty-nine-year-old music teacher of 20 Leveson Street, was much liked by her neighbours. She was an amiable and pleasant young woman, a mother of two children; five-year-old, Henry George and three-year-old, John Alfred.

In the winter of 1849, Ann discovered that she was pregnant once again. Her Danish mariner husband, John Hinrichson, was elated at the news and looked forward to being present at the birth of his third child, after he had completed a voyage on his ship, the *Duncan*. Mr Hinrichson was not to know that he would never see his unborn child, or his wife and boys again, for fate was about to deal him a cruel hand in the spring of that year.

In March 1849, Mrs Hinrichson awoke to a severe bout of morning sickness. She was attended by her young maidservant, Mary Parr, a conscientious and indispensable girl, who lessened Mrs Hinrichson's tasks of running the household. As well as being a servant, Miss Parr had also become a very trustworthy friend.

After breakfast, Mrs Hinrichson placed a cardboard notice in the front parlour window of her three-storey home. The card read: 'Furnished Apartments to let'. The pregnant music teacher was a very naive woman in the ways of the world, and she confidently told Miss Parr that it would not be long before someone decent responded to the notice and applied for lodgings. Leveson Street in those days ran from Great George Street to Suffolk Street, and it was a busy thoroughfare. Hundreds of passers-by probably glanced at the card in the window of number 20, but only one of them called in to inspect the vacant rooms, and this individual, John Gleeson Wilson, was a twenty-six-year-old Irishman from Limerick.

Wilson knocked on the door and Mary Parr answered. Wilson

asked if he could view the vacant rooms and was shown the front parlour and the back bedroom. Finding the accommodation to his liking, he immediately paid a week's rent in advance and moved in. The Irishman claimed to be a carpenter, employed by the Dock Estate, and Mrs Hinrichson was pleased at having such an upright and hard-working young man as a lodger. What she did not know, was that Wilson already had lodgings in Porter Street, off Great Howard Street.

That night, at around ten o'clock, Mr Wilson said goodnight to Mrs Hinrichson and retired to his bed. On the following morning he rose early, and by seven-thirty he was in a nearby pub in Great George Street, having a glass of ale for breakfast. At this public house, the first move that would lead to the wholesale slaughter of four innocent people took place. Wilson asked the pub's landlady if she could provide him with a wafer to seal an envelope containing an important letter.

"No, I'm sorry dear," she said. "But I've got a stick of sealing wax. Will that do?"

"Yes," answered Wilson.

The woman brought him the sealing wax and watched him use it to fix down the flap of the envelope. Wilson then asked the landlady if she would be so kind as to write the address on the envelope, as he could not write. The pub proprietress blushed red with embarrassment.

"I can't write either," she confided in a whisper, and she called for her daughter, Nora.

Nora was a bright girl who compiled the inventory at the pub. The landlady asked the girl to write the address on the customer's envelope. Nora proudly fetched her pen and pot of ink. John Wilson dictated the address and Nora inscribed it on the envelope with artistic swirling strokes. The calligraphy was beautiful. The address ran: 'John Wilson, Esq, 20 Leveson Street, Liverpool'.

Without further ado, Wilson kissed Nora's knuckle and left the pub. He called to a passing schoolboy and asked him if he wanted to earn a few pennies by simply delivering a letter.

"Yes, sir!" the child nodded enthusiastically.

In his charming Irish brogue, Wilson explained what the boy was to do to earn his payment.

"When I go into the house [in Leveson Street], I want you to wait a few minutes, and then I want you to knock. Then I want you to ask the person who comes to the door if John Wilson lives there. Have you got that?"

"John Wilson," the boy repeated, and struggled to remember the name.

"Tell the person who comes to the door that you have a letter for John Wilson from his employer," Wilson continued, speaking slowly and clearly so that the lad would absorb the information.

"From his employer," echoed the schoolboy.

"Got that then?" Wilson asked, and briefly ran through his instructions again.

The boy insisted that he knew what to say, and Wilson handed him the letter, before going into 20 Leveson Street.

About a minute later, the schoolboy hurried to number 20 and hammered on the brass knocker.

Mary Parr answered, "Yes?" she said curtly, seeing the urchin on the step.

"Does – does Mr John Wilson live here?" the youth inquired, as instructed, and fidgeted nervously with the letter he was brandishing.

"Yes, here he is."

Miss Parr stepped aside, into the vestibule, and allowed John Wilson to come to the door.

"What is it?" Wilson asked, and winked at the boy.

"Here's a letter from your employer, sir."

The schoolchild thrust the letter at Wilson and then watched him rummage in his pocket. Instead of paying him immediately, Wilson went back into the house for a moment, and returned with a few pennies borrowed from Mrs Hinrichson. He gave the coppers to the gleeful boy, who turned and ran off to buy sweets. Wilson then returned to his room clutching the letter which he had sent to himself.

The whole object of the subterfuge was to create the impression that Wilson was employed by the Dock Estate, which of course was not true at all. He was unemployed.

That morning, at eleven o'clock, Mrs Hinrichson visited the greengrocers in St James Street and ordered a basketful of potatoes. She then called at a chandlers to purchase two large jugs, which she asked to be delivered to her home. She then returned to her house.

That was the last time she was seen alive.

Early in the afternoon, an errand boy arrived at 20 Leveson Street with the potatoes. Wilson came to the door and took the vegetables from the boy. He returned a short time later with the empty basket and closed the door. He had seemed quite calm.

Half an hour later, the delivery boy from the chandler's shop arrived at the Hinrichson's home with the newly-purchased jugs. He rang the doorbell repeatedly but received no answer. He lifted the knocker and three times he brought it down as hard as he could. Still no one came to the door, so the delivery boy took a squinting peek through the keyhole of the front door. What he saw made him gasp with horror, because he could clearly see a pair of legs lying across the hallway. The boy's macabre imagination was aroused by the sight, and his grim curiosity inspired him to climb the railings in front of the parlour window.

Perched on top of the railings, he was able to view the inside of the dim front parlour, and he nearly toppled over when he beheld the sickening sight inside the room, which was like an abattoir, with blood splattered everywhere. In scarlet pools lay the bodies of Mary Parr and little Henry George Hinrichson. The errand boy shuddered and jumped down from the railings, feeling numb with shock. What if the killer came after him, now that he had witnessed his terrible deeds? The boy was too terrified to look back as he fled the scene in panic, abandoning the two jugs on the doorstep. He ran until he had a stitch in his side, and eventually stumbled into the arms of a policeman who was walking his beat in St George's Street.

"What's to do, lad?" asked the policeman, wondering who the boy was running from.

"Murder," the child muttered faintly, all out of breath. He took in a gulp of air and tried again. "Murder!" he cried.

"Oi! Now then, son. That isn't funny," the policeman said, in a serious voice, feeling that his authority was being undermined.

The boy earnestly assured the policeman that he was not joking, and urged him to go with him to the house in Leveson Street, to see the bodies for himself. So the policeman and the youngster made their way back towards the Hinrichson household.

Meanwhile, a young girl, who was a regular pupil of Mrs Hinrichson, was arriving at the house for a music lesson. After getting no reply, and seeing the jugs on the doorstep, the girl went next door to the neighbour, a Mr Hughes, and told him that she thought something might be wrong. Mr Hughes hammered on the door several times, then looked through the parlour window's upper panes. After seeing the same scenes of carnage that had sent the errand boy running for the police, Mr Hughes broke a window pane and made a forced entry into the house. Within minutes, other people from the street were swarming into number 20. By the time the policeman and the errand boy arrived on the scene, almost every inhabitant of Leveson Street was milling about outside the house of horror.

Later that afternoon, the police swarmed to Leveson Street

and carried out a thorough search of the premises. The first body which the police investigators had encountered was that of Ann Hinrichson. She was lying in the hallway. Her head had been smashed in, revealing brain matter. Several deep stab wounds had penetrated her chest and abdomen. The killer had made sure that he had finished her off, and had thereby unknowingly killed the unborn child in her womb as well. There was so much blood around the body, that one policeman slipped and fell in the clotting mire.

In the parlour they came upon the body of Mary Parr, the maid. Her hair was a sticky matted mass of blood. A detective flinched at the gaping head wound. The victim still had a faint pulse, but was barely alive. She was carefully laid on a stretcher and taken to the Southern Hospital.

Five-year-old Henry George was not so lucky. His eyes gazed lifelessly up at the ceiling, a look of terror still etched on his innocent, young face. His head and clothes were streaked with blood from the savage assault.

Down in the cellar, the police found the body of his younger brother, John Alfred Hinrichson, aged just three. His angelic little mouth formed a small oval from the scream he had obviously made as the killer callously slit his throat from ear to ear. One policeman was so overcome with grief at the sight of the slaughtered child, that he left the house in tears and was sent home. Even the hard-boiled detectives were shaken at the killer's handywork.

What sort of person would carry out such a cowardly series of killings? And what could his motive possibly be? A bowl of bloodstained water was found in Wilson's room, along with a poker and tongs that were dappled with blood. It was later established that a large sum of money, belonging to the absent husband John Hinrichson, had gone missing.

Mary Parr regained consciousness at the hospital and found

herself encircled by policemen and detectives. The girl managed to recount the horrific nightmare that had taken place in the house that afternoon, then she slipped into a coma.

Sightings of the killer were soon reported. The murderer had, for some unfathomable reason gone straight to Toxteth Park, to wash his blood-spattered clothes in the figure-of-eight-shaped pit. From the park he had then made his way to a pawnbrokers in London Road, where he had sold a gold watch. The money from the sale was then used to purchase a pair of trousers from a tailor in Great Homer Street. From there, the killer went to his other lodgings, in northern Liverpool, at Porter Street. Wilson had the audacity to ask his landlady to wash his blood-stained shirt, and the woman naturally became suspicious when she saw the state of her lodger's garment.

That same evening, at six o'clock, Wilson called at a barber's shop round the corner from his lodgings and requested a shave. While the barber was lathering his face, Wilson casually asked him if he happened to have a wig to sell. The bemused barber replied that he had not and wondered why his customer should want one, as he had such a fine head of red hair. Wilson insisted that he needed a toupé, so the barber told him that there was a wigmaker who specialised in men's hairpieces in Oil Street, which was only three streets away. After he had shaved Wilson, the barber took him round to the shop. During the short walk to Oil Street, Wilson casually asked, "Have you heard about the murder?"

"No, what murder is that?" the barber inquired.

"A terrible affair," Wilson replied. "Two women and two children had their heads bashed in."

"How awful!" the barber commented, shaking his head in disgust. "Did they get him?"

"No, not yet," said Wilson.

After purchasing a wig, Wilson took a ferry ride across the

Mersey and went to Tranmere to spend the night with his estranged wife. On the following morning, John Gleeson Wilson did something which was inexplicably stupid, given his situation. Despite being fully aware that a police dragnet had been thrown over Liverpool to snare the most wanted man in Europe, Wilson boarded a ferry and returned to the city. He visited the shop of Mr Israel Samuel, a Great Howard Street watch dealer. Mr Samuel was an astute and intuitive man, and he felt uneasy about Wilson, who wanted six pounds for another gold watch. Mr Samuel called for a policeman and asked him to examine the watch. The constable assured him that the timepiece did not resemble any watch that had been reported stolen. Still, there was something about Mr Wilson that Israel Samuel could not put his finger on. Something strange in the man's pale blue eyes; something suspicious about his erratic gestures. Mr Samuel told Wilson that he would buy the watch, but had insufficient cash on the premises at the time to pay him. Wilson angrily snatched back the watch and was just about to leave, when Mr Samuel called, "Wait! If you would like go with my son to my other shop, in Dale Street, he will give you the money there."

Wilson halted and sullenly nodded in agreement.

Mr Samuel then said to his son in Hebrew: "When you are passing the police station near Dale Street, collar this fellow and hand him over."

Mr Samuel's son did just as his father had instructed. As he walked up Dale Street with Wilson, he grabbed him and pinned his arm up his back, then pushed him up Cheapside to the bridewell. Wilson had been off guard and was totally taken by surprise.

Around this time, Miss Mary Parr, the Hinrichson's maidservant, died in hospital without regaining consciousness.

After a lengthy interrogation session, Wilson was charged with the murders and thrown into a cell at the bridewell. In the days leading up to his trial, he often took fits of rage and screamed out that he was innocent.

He was tried at Liverpool Assizes on 23 August 1849, before Mr Justice Patterson. Without leaving their box, the jury found Wilson guilty of the four murders. John Wilson, who, it transpired, was actually named Maurice Gleeson Wilson, was sentenced to death.

On the sunny Saturday morning of 15 September 1849, a crowd of some fifty thousand people from all over the Northwest of England gathered to watch the execution of Wilson, at Kirkdale Gaol. At around 11.30am, the vast crowds became eerily silent as a white dove descended from the azure heavens and landed on the crossbeam of the scaffold. The bird perched there, eyeing the mob for a while, until it was startled into flight by the approach of two men; the prison governor and a priest. The governor had come into the prison yard to explain the workings of the scaffold to the priest, who wanted to be reassured that the condemned man would have a swift and humane death.

Shortly before noon, Wilson was escorted by the Under Sheriff from the condemned cell to the press room to meet the public executioner; a seventy-year-old hangman from York, by the name of Howard. Mr Howard had a record of incompetence, and seemed more nervous than the condemned man himself. He fumbled clumsily with the straps as he bound the Irishman's hand and foot.

Wilson was escorted outside to the scaffold by two priests who recited the Litany for the Dying. Wilson's face was now very pallid, and he too was whispering a prayer. Close behind him was the executioner, who was now displaying a prominent nervous twitch in his face.

Wilson was manoeuvred back and forth as the executioner positioned him on the drop. Mr Howard grumbled to himself as he awkwardly slipped the noose over Wilson's head in the wrong position. He then adjusted the noose so that the knot was on the right side of his neck. Howard then produced the white cap and shook it. He tried to pull it down over Wilson's head, but realised, too late, that the cap was too small. He then angrily tried to force it down over Wilson's face, but it only covered the condemned man's eyebrows and he eventually abandoned the task, leaving Wilson to witness his own execution.

The crowd grew excited as the executioner stood back for a moment and surveyed Wilson's position on the scaffold. Howard's trembling arm then reached for the release lever. The clergymen standing on each side of Wilson backed away slowly, still reciting prayers. Anticipating the final moments of Wilson's life, the holy men raised their voices as they prayed for the ill-fated mass murderer.

Howard triggered the mechanism that drew the bolt back with a dramatic thud – but the Leveson Street psychopath fell a mere two feet. A tremendous cheer went up from the crowd, which faded rapidly as the spectators witnessed the final throes of Wilson's terrible death.

The incompetent Howard should have made the drop much longer than twenty-four inches. Despite the assurances to the priests, Wilson's death was not swift at all. Because of the executioner's lack of skill, Maurice Gleeson Wilson drew up his legs in spasm, and because the white cap was not pulled over his grossly contorted face, some faint-hearted onlookers at the front of the crowd swooned, while others screamed in shock and horror. Wilson's eyes bulged out of their sockets, and veins like purple knotted cords sprang up from his bulging crimson cheeks. His elongated tongue lolled grotesquely out of his foaming, gasping mouth, and he started to make the most gut-wrenching choking sounds. Howard panicked and ran over to the hanging man and started to desperately tug at the white cap, in an effort to cover his face which betrayed his agony, and Howard's incompetence. Wilson's protruding eyes glanced sideways at the executioner in silent accusation, until Howard managed to yank the cap down over them. The choking sound continued for about fifteen seconds, then the body stopped struggling to fight the onset of slow strangulation.

Ann Hinrichson, her unborn child and two young sons were buried, along with Mary Parr, in the same grave in St James' Cemetery. Because of the notorious massacre associated with Leveson Street, crowds of morbid individuals made regular pilgrimages to see the house of blood at number 20. To dissuade the ghoulish sightseers from visiting the infamous street, the council later renamed the thoroughfare Grenville Street. Today, Grenville Street South is the only surviving vestige of a street that was once synonymous with brutal mass murder.

Mad or Bad?

Frederick Bailey Deeming was born in Birkenhead in 1853, the youngest child of a poverty-stricken couple's seven children. In his teens, like so many young men before him, he abandoned his family for a life at sea, working as ship's steward. He travelled the world and, for some unknown reason, began to adopt several aliases such as Lawson, Duncan, Druin and Williams, to mention but a few.

On his voyages around the globe he was alleged to have stopped off in various countries to perpetrate a series of murders and frauds. On several occasions, the undeniably handsome blue-eyed, wavy-haired Deeming entered into marriage for financial gain, killed his wife and quickly moved on with the proceeds. There is also evidence that Deeming once knifed a

Zulu to death over some dispute in the South African Cape, and on another occasion, he shot thirteen lions in a day, to satisfy an incredible bloodlust which he was developing. Much has been written about the potent drive to kill that was motivating Deeming at this time. Was it inherent, or could there have been a physiological reason behind the impetus to murder and maim? The brain has an aggression centre called the amygdaloid nucleus, and should this pea-sized portion of the cerebrum become affected by hormonal changes, tumour, or even alcohol, a person can suddenly develop an uncontrollable urge to kill.

A case in point was Charles Whitman, a twenty-five-year-old American marine. In August 1966, Whitman complained of severe headaches, and began to act oddly, breaking into fits of uncontrollable violence. He sought psychiatric counselling, but his mother and his wife simply attributed his behaviour change to stress. On 31 July, Whitman wrote a note which read: 'I am prepared to die. After my death, I wish an autopsy to be performed on me, to see if there is any mental disorder.' That night, he stabbed and shot his mother to death at her house and then returned home, where he stabbed his wife to death and wrote a diatribe against his abusive father, which closed with the words: 'Life is not worth living'.

On the morning of 1 August 1966, Charles Whitman packed sandwiches, toilet paper, a transistor radio, a can of Spam, a jar of Planters Peanuts, a tin of fruit cocktail, a box of raisins, jerricans containing water and gasoline, rope, binoculars, canteens, a plastic bottle of Mennen spray deodorant and an arsenal of weapons, including a 6mm Remington bolt-action rifle, a 35mm Remington rifle, a Galesi-Brescia pistol, a .357 Magnum Smith & Wesson revolver, a .30 calibre carbine, a 12-gauge sawn-off shotgun and over seven hundred rounds of ammunition. He then headed for the University of Texas campus and climbed to the top of the thirty storey clock tower with a mission: to gun down everything and everybody that moved.

As he got to the top of the tower, Charles smashed in the skull of a receptionist with his rifle and shot dead two tourists, that he encountered in the stairwell, at point-blank range. He then set up a sniper's nest and began shooting people at random. Hundreds of people were strolling around the large college campus that afternoon and as the first shots rang out, and bodies began to drop, the entire college was frozen in panic and fear.

In ninety-nine minutes of shooting, Charles Whitman killed fifteen people and wounded thirty-one, some at distances of one thousand yards. Police were unable to hit him from the ground, so finally they decided to storm the tower and made their way to the roof, where they charged through Whitman's barricade. Charles fired at the police who, in turn, fired back. In the end, Charles Whitman lay dead – felled by three Austin patrolmen and a retired Air Force tail-gunner.

As requested by Whitman in the note he left, an autopsy was performed, and revealed a golfball-sized tumour located in the hypothalamus region of the brain. It had been pressing on the amygdaloid nucleus – which is directly connected with violent behaviour and altered judgement.

Perhaps Frederick Deeming was suffering from such a condition, or perhaps he was simply evil. When the black-hearted seafarer gave up his maritime occupation and returned home, he found employment as a plumber and he also found himself a pretty young lady named Marie James, who instantly fell for Deeming's good looks and soon married him. Marie bore him four children, but Deeming later callously abandoned his wife and children and went across the Mersey seeking a new life and a new love.

In July 1891, Deeming took the lease of a cottage called Dinham Villa at Rainhill, near St Helens, where he posed as an army inspector named Albert Williams, who was supposedly acting on the behalf of a Colonel Brooks. It was not long before Emily Mather, the landlady's twenty-five-year-old daughter, took an admiring interest in dashing Deeming, and suddenly there was romance in the air. Pretty young Emily was enthralled by Deeming's colourful tales of his seafaring days and the dewy-eyed girl confided to her closest friends that she had met Mr Right at last.

Then Deeming's abandoned wife and family turned up, unannounced, at the villa. With amazing composure, the unruffled Deeming casually passed Marie off as his sister. Infatuated Emily believed the tale, and Deeming realised that drastic action was now required to lend some credibility to his story. Marie and the children had to be disposed of. Deeming went out to buy a pick-axe and several bags of cement, then he waited for the right moment to arise, which came during the night, when his wife and four children were sleeping soundly in their beds.

Wearing nothing but his nightshirt, Deeming crept into his family's bedroom clutching a cut-throat razor. He stealthily approached the bed of the first child and pressed his heavy hand over the boy's peaceful cherubic face. He took care not to move the boy too much as he carved a gaping slit across his small throat. The boy's body soon became limp, as arterial blood sprayed over Deeming's razor-wielding fist. The psychopathic father then moved onto the next child and repeated the same horrific procedure. When he came to his two daughters, he slashed the neck of one, but for some reason decided to strangle the other. The girl's eyes flew open and she gazed in startled confusion as her poker-faced father gripped her throat and began to crush her slender neck. After strangling her to death, he then also cut his wife's throat from ear to ear.

The next grisly task he performed was the entombment of the bodies. He hid the five corpses in the shallow graves which he had created under the hearthstones of the kitchen floor, and later employed labourers to assist him in cementing over the kitchen's uneven flags. Deeming accomplished this by explaining that Colonel Brooks hated uneven floors. So, unknowingly, the workmen helped entomb the only obstacles that had stood in the way of Deeming's calculated romance with Miss Mather. When the newly-surfaced kitchen floor finally dried out, Deeming threw a party and invited his sweetheart, Emily, and several other guests. During the merrymaking, Deeming callously danced with the unsuspecting guests upon the graves of his wife and children. Later that evening he got down on his bended knee and proposed to Emily Mather. She accepted with a coy smile and a slight blush and the couple married at St Anne's Church, Rainhill, on 22 September 1891.

Shortly after the marriage, Deeming became intensely uneasy about living at Dinham Villa. He feared that his slowly decomposing victims would start to smell, so he told Emily that he was vacating the house because the 'Colonel' had changed his mind about occupying it. Deeming left the villa and moved into his new wife's home, half a mile away. However, he soon started to get itchy feet again, and told Emily that, as an Inspector of Regiments, he had received correspondence from the British Army, requesting him to be stationed in Windsor, Australia.

On 15 December, Deeming and his wife arrived in Melbourne and travelled out to the city's suburban district of Windsor, where they rented a cottage at 57 Andrew Street. The couple unpacked their bags, and Emily was quite content to make a new life 'Down Under', but already, Deeming was planning the next shocking move in his infamous career.

Nine days after moving into the cottage, he picked up an axe and brought it down heavily on Emily's head six times, smashing her skull like an eggshell. After the first blow, the young woman's legs collapsed with shock, and Deeming then proceeded mercilessly to reduce her head to a pulpy mass. To be certain that life was extinct, Deeming knelt down and, with a sawing movement using his long-bladed knife to cut deeply into Emily's throat, he severed the jugular vein, windpipe and other tissues as far as the spine. Once again, in a repetition of his earlier crime, up came the hearthstone, that was shortly to become Emily's headstone.

Early in the following year, Deeming packed his bags again and boarded a Sydney-bound steamer. On board the ship he met a beautiful young woman named Kate Rounsfell, and before the steamer had reached Sydney Harbour, he had won her heart. He proposed to her and offered her an impressive diamond ring, but Kate was not hasty at accepting the offer of marriage. Nevertheless, she decided she wanted to get to know Deeming better. He told her that he was intending to join the gold rush in Western Australia, and that he would soon be a very wealthy man. Still interested, Kate Rounsfell was not yet sure about the commitment of marriage, but said she would follow Deeming.

Meanwhile, back in Melbourne, a woman was enquiring about the vacant house at 57 Andrew Street. The landlord of the premises accompanied the prospective tenant to the empty house and allowed her to inspect the place. In the bedroom, they encountered the terrible stench of Emily's rotting corpse. The unscrupulous landlord claimed the smell was merely from dead mice, but the woman promptly left, feeling nauseous. With the help of another man, the landlord traced the awful smell to the hearthstone in the bedroom and together they lifted it up. The aroma of decaying tissue suddenly became totally overpowering.

The police were informed, and when they later broke up a layer of newly-laid cement under the bedroom floor, they discovered the hollowed-out grave containing the doubled-up body of a woman. Police inquiries established that the name of the last tenant at the house of horror had been a 'Mr Druin', who had mysteriously left without giving any notice. During a thorough search of the house the police found a luggage ticket, and traced it to a shipping clerk who recalled booking a sea passage for a man who called himself 'Baron Swanston'.

The police in Melbourne lost no time in cabling the information to their colleagues in Perth. There, Detective George Gurney made further inquiries and discovered that a Baron Swanston had stayed at the city's Shamrock Hotel, and what is more, he had left a forwarding address – a house at Southern Cross, in the Western Australian Outback. Gurney quickly telegraphed the police outpost at Southern Cross, and on the following morning, two armed constables rode to Fraser's Gold Mine and arrested Deeming. He reacted with outraged innocence, protesting that it was all a terrible mistake.

He was bundled into a mail coach and the two hundred mile journey to Perth commenced. During the long journey to justice, news broke of the horrendous discovery of Deeming's butchered family at Dinham Villa in Rainhill, England. Shortly afterwards, Kate Rounsfell, who was on her way to meet her fiancé, received a telegram from her frantic sister, warning her not to proceed any further. Kate almost fainted when she realised that she would, almost certainly, have been Deeming's next victim.

While awaiting trial, Deeming spent most of his time making morbid sketches of gallows and reading from the Bible. Then a rumour circulated the prison which alleged that he had confessed to being Jack the Ripper! In reality, Deeming was not even in London at the time of the Whitechapel murders, but still, the newspapers had a field day with the unfounded claims, and the *Melbourne Evening Standard* soon ran the sensational headline: 'Jack the Ripper: Deeming at Aldgate on the night of the Whitechapel Murders'.

The murder trial opened on 8 May, 1892 at Melbourne

Criminal Court. Deeming was tried for killing his wife, Emily, but had not been charged with the Rainhill murders, as they had taken place in England. Deeming's defence counsel was a young barrister named Alfred Deakin, who would later become Australia's Prime Minister on three occasions. Deakin argued eloquently and persuasively that Deeming was insane, and so could not be held responsible for his actions. But his rhetoric was useless. On the final day of the trial, Deeming obtained the court's permission to address the jury, and for a whole hour he maintained that he had not been given a fair trial, as the newspapers had already made up people's minds for them.

However, his appeal was in vain; after thirty minutes of deliberation, the jury returned a guilty verdict. On the sunny morning of 23 May 1892, Frederick Deeming walked to the scaffold, puffing on a large cigar given to him by the prison warder. By now, the serial killer's hair had turned snow white.

Seconds before the hangman threw the lever, Deeming whispered, "Lord receive my spirit". Then he plunged through the trap-door and struggled, kicked and made choking sounds for a short while. The noose had broken his neck, but the nerves in his body caused him to twitch and act in a lifelike way for a while.

After the execution, pathologists sawed open Deeming's skull, and dissected his brains, dissecting the grey matter to see if they could pinpoint some physiological reason for the killer's behaviour. The nineteenth century neurologists and criminologists could not agree on the causes of Deeming's behaviour. A plaster cast of the killer's head was made and copies of this deathmask were sent to Scotland Yard and sold to private collectors. One copy of the gruesome deathmask was exhibited at Reynold's Waxworks, in Liverpool's Lime Street for a number of years.

Flogged

At 62 Rodney Street, there is a plaque which reads: 'Gladstone, Four times Prime Minister, born in this house, 29th December 1809'.

William Ewart Gladstone was an impressive reformer, legislator and legendary orator, who dominated politics alongside his Conservative opponent, Benjamin Disraeli. Gladstone's reforming legislation included Cardwell's Army reform of 1868, which supposedly made peacetime flogging illegal. However, a particularly nasty flogging incident took place in 1877, when thirty-eight-year-old Margaret McCann, of Mill Street, Toxteth, was punished by two dockside labourers for burglary.

Mrs McCann's wrists were securely tied to railings in a court off Prince William Street. Her chemise was ripped off, exposing her back, and in full view of a policeman, the two dockers took turns to whip her with their belts until the woman fainted. The belt buckles had flailed the skin off Mrs McCann's back, leaving the whole of it a bloody mess. Two policemen later interviewed the vigilantes, but no charges were brought against them, and there were accusations of police bribery.

Margaret McCann recovered sufficiently to later resort to violence herself. In 1880, she attacked her neighbour, Margaret Neiles, with a hatchet in her home at Hyslop Street, Toxteth. The hatchet blade hacked seven serious wounds into Mrs Neiles' body, including a deep, five-inch gash in her forehead. As her victim slumped to the floor, in a semi-conscious state, with blood spurting from her horrific wounds, Mrs McCann's husband joined in the carnage, by battering Mrs Neiles with a hefty wooden mallet. The victim already had a severely fractured skull from the hatchet onslaught, but Mr McCann proceeded to rain several heavy blows on her anyway.

Mrs Neiles was rushed to hospital and, against the odds, later made a miraculous recovery. Her attackers were subsequently gaoled. Margaret McCann was ordered to serve twelve years' penal servitude. The trial judge declared that he could show no leniency, not only because of the savagery of the attack, but also because Mrs McCann had already served six sentences for serious assault.

In 1855, in the cruel days before Gladstone outlawed peacetime flogging, an elderly woman named Mrs Derry was brutally whipped for organising the theft of ten loaves of bread. This was during the bread riots of February 1855, when most of the bread and flour shops of Liverpool were plundered by starving mobsup to several thousand strong. A former soldier named Gunnison, and a baker named Crosbie, caught some of the thieves red-handed, as they were helping themselves to loaves from a bakery in Dale Street. The thieves managed to escape, but Mrs Derry, a frail old woman in her seventies, was allegedly caught and whipped across the face with a riding crop by Gunnison. The poor woman never recovered from the brutal punishment and died some weeks later from delayed shock.

No charges were brought against Gunnison, who was a notorious sadist, because the Mayor, JA Tobin – who was on the verge of declaring a state of martial law in Liverpool – was a good friend of his. Trade was brought to a virtual standstill and businesses had to close as the bread riots worsened. The Mayor was ultimately forced to feed the city's poor, by raising large sums of money to buy loaves.

Lucky Escape

She was a pretty, young, auburn-haired woman from Mobile, Alabama, and he was a wealthy middle-aged businessman from the respectable suburb of Aigburth. She was eighteen-year-old Florence Chandler, and he was forty-two-year-old James Maybrick, and it was upon the luxurious White Star liner, *Britannic*, in the year 1881, when their respective paths through life crossed.

As the Liverpool-bound liner cut through the icy expanses of the mid-Atlantic, James Maybrick first set eyes upon Miss Chandler, who was travelling alone on the voyage. He approached her and introduced himself, and when she spoke in reply, Mr Maybrick found her accent quaintly indeterminable. It seemed to contain elements of upper-class English, a hint of the continental, together with intonations of the American Deep South. Miss Chandler explained that her hybrid accent was the result of a cosmopolitan upbringing. During her formative years she had lived with various relatives in London, Paris and other major European cities, as well as New York, where she had just been to visit her grandmother. The vestiges of Florence's southern drawl were the legacy of a childhood spent amongst the sunny cotton fields of Alabama.

When Maybrick mentioned that he was from Liverpool, Miss Chandler told him that she had once been to the city, to see the world-famous Grand National at Aintree, and she began to talk of horsemanship which, by a coincidence, was one of Mr Maybrick's main interests.

Seven days later, James Maybrick proudly announced his engagement to Miss Chandler to the rest of the liner's passengers, and when the captain of the *Britannic* learned of the betrothal, he rang the ship's bell in celebration and proposed a toast to the couple's future.

They seemed like the perfect couple and later that year, in July, the two were married in London, at St James' Church, Piccadilly, after which they enjoyed an exotic honeymoon in Brazil.

For several years the couple lived in Norfolk, Virginia, where Mr Maybrick, as a cotton broker, conducted his business. Every morning he would leave Mrs Maybrick – who by now had a baby boy to look after – and head for his office at the Norfolk Cotton Exchange. Unknown to his wife, James Maybrick did not always go directly to work after kissing her goodbye. On most mornings he made little detours to various drug stores along Main Street to purchase arsenic, which he took regularly in small quantities, because, for some reason, he believed it fortified him.

On one occasion, Maybrick was preparing a meal for himself, when a friend observed him adding a quantity of grey powder to the food. When Maybrick's friend asked him what the powder was, he casually replied, "It is arsenic. We all take some poison more or less. For instance, I am now taking enough arsenic to kill you. I take this once in a while, because I find it strengthens me."

In 1884, the Maybricks returned to England and took up residence at Battlecrease House, in Aigburth's Riversdale Road. James Maybrick continued to prosper in his business, and he and Florence moved upwards into the exclusive circles of Liverpool's high society. They attended countless soirées, dances, dinner parties and horse races, as well as numerous important public events held at St George's Hall.

In 1886, Florence Maybrick gave birth to a second child, a daughter named Gladys Evelyn, but the joy which the new child brought was dramatically cut short, when an epidemic of scarlatina hit Liverpool. Five-year-old James Maybrick, the elder child, was stricken with the fever. His father feared that his baby daughter would also contract the deadly disease, so he and a nursemaid took her to Wales, leaving Florence to nurse little

James. For six long, anxious weeks Florence tended to her son, and in the end, thanks to her untiring dedication, he pulled through. However, around this time, Florence was devastated to learn from one of her staff at Battlecrease House, that her apparently devoted husband kept a mistress somewhere in Liverpool, and that, long before his marriage to her, this woman had given birth to two of his children. Worse still, since the marriage, the woman had borne James Maybrick a third child, Florence was horrified to learn.

When James Maybrick returned to Battlecrease House, Florence decided not to confront him over his extra-marital relationship, but instead acted as if everything were perfectly normal. Not that her husband would have noticed anyway. He started to stay out late, and often told Florence that he would be going to London on business, but she found she could no longer trust him. She spent many interminable lonely nights sitting in the drawing room, wondering where her husband really was and what he was doing. He had increasingly become a stranger to her. Then, one night when he returned home, Florence told him that she could no longer bring herself to sleep in the same bed as him.

In December 1888, the Maybricks were entertaining a number of guests at their home, and one guest in particular viewed Florence with an amorous eye. He was a tall, handsome, thirty-eight-year-old bachelor named Alfred Brierley, also a wealthy cotton broker, who had offices in both New Orleans and Liverpool, and who came from a prominent Lancashire family. Standing head and shoulders above the other guests, Brierley quickly caught the attention of Florence, who found him very charming.

Brierley was invited back to the house many times and became a frequent dinner guest at the home of the Maybricks. During the following March, Brierley often accompanied James and

Florence to the early spring horse races. As the weeks passed by, it became patently obvious that Florence was becoming increasingly fond of Brierley, and vice versa. While James Maybrick was away in London on business, Alfred Brierley visited Florence and declared his love for her. He asked her to go away with him. Florence tried hard to hold back her feelings for a while, but then relented. She later spent three days – and nights – with Brierley at Flatman's Hotel in London's Cavendish Square, posing as his wife.

Florence returned from her little sojourn on 28 March, and on the following day she accompanied her husband to Aintree Race Course for the Grand National. Among the crowd of racegoers that day was Alfred Brierley. As they caught sight of him, Florence blushed and gave Brierley a little tell-tale smile, which drove her husband wild with jealousy. To make matters worse, Brierley approached the Maybricks and, after exchanging formal greetings with both of them, asked Florence if she would like to go and see the Prince of Wales. Florence needed no second invitation. She nodded enthusiastically and took his arm. The two smiled at each other under the cover of Florence's parasol and walked off towards the grandstand, leaving Maybrick speechless with anger.

Later that day, back at Battlecrease House, James Maybrick gave his wife a black eye during a fierce altercation over the Brierley incident, and Florence decided that enough was enough. She announced that she was leaving him immediately, but James warned her that if she did leave him, he would never allow her to see the children again. At this, Florence reluctantly walked back into the hall, confused and dismayed, and Maybrick roared, "By heavens, Florrie, if you cross this doorstep you shall never enter this house again!"

At this, Mrs Maybrick broke down, silently crying at the finality of the harsh ultimatum. Without speaking, she turned on her heel, as the tears streamed down her cheeks and the children's nursemaid led Florence to the nursery, where the baby was also crying.

On the following morning, Florence sought the advice of the family physician, Dr Arthur Hopper. She related to him, in broken tones, the details of her husband's brutal attack on her, and, as Dr Hopper examined her blackened eye, she told him that she intended to see if a separation could be arranged. The doctor tried to dissuade her from such a drastic course of action, and he promised that he would drop in at Battlecrease House to remonstrate with Mr Maybrick about the deplorable wife-beating incident.

About a week afterwards, Alfred Brierley received a letter from Florence, urging him to visit her without delay. When Brierley arrived, he was shocked to see that Florence was sporting a grotesque-looking, swollen black eye. In some distress, she told him about the beating which she had received after returning from the Grand National. Although Brierley was visibly upset by the evidence of the barbaric treatment that Florence had endured at the hands of her violently jealous husband, he offered no remedy to the situation, and no support whatsoever. This was yet another bitter blow to Florence.

On 13 April, James Maybrick boarded a train for London, where he intended to spend the weekend with his brother, Michael, before consulting a Dr Charles Fuller about the state of his health. Maybrick was something of a hypochondriac and held the deep-seated but unfounded belief that every ache and pain he suffered heralded the onset of creeping paralysis. Ironically, most of the health problems he experienced were being caused by the arsenical medications which he was forever taking for his imaginary disease.

Dr Fuller carried out a very thorough examination of Maybrick, after which he informed him that his symptoms indicated nothing more serious than dyspepsia, a mild digestive problem. Maybrick was very relieved to receive this diagnosis, and returned to Liverpool in an optimistic mood on 22 April.

A couple of days after his arrival back in Liverpool, the local chemist, Thomas Wokes, received a visit from Florence Maybrick and she purchased a dozen fly-papers. She complained to Mr Wokes that the flies in the kitchen were multiplying. Mr Wokes smiled and rolled the fly-papers up and handed them to the delivery boy. Mrs Maybrick paid him sixpence and then returned home, ahead of the delivery boy.

Several days later, two servants were curious to observe a towel covering something in Mrs Maybrick's room. One of them lifted the towel and saw a basin underneath. In the basin was a small bowl, also covered by a towel. The curious servant could not resist peeping under this towel and found several fly-papers soaking in a bowl of water. In those days, fly-papers contained significant amounts of arsenic, and the servants, aware of this, exchanged knowing glances.

Two days later, James Maybrick was coming downstairs when he experienced a distressing spell of dizziness. After the spell lifted, Maybrick proceeded to his office in the city. He arrived at the Knowsley Buildings shortly after 10.30am and he complained to his colleagues of stiffness in his legs. That afternoon, Maybrick tried to shake off his symptoms by carrying on as normal and he went across the Mersey to see some horse races on the Wirral. When he arrived, his face was a livid, sickly white, and several racetrack friends commented on how poorly he looked.

By the time Maybrick arrived home at Battlecrease House, he was sweating profusely and so went straight to bed. When he awoke the next morning, he found his condition was just the same, so Dr Humphreys – who was the children's physician, and the doctor who lived nearest to the house – was summoned.

When the doctor arrived, Mrs Maybrick told him about the white powder her husband had a habit of taking, and the doctor quizzed Maybrick about his arsenic addiction.

Later that day, Mr Maybrick's health improved slightly, and he was able to enjoy a bowl of oxtail soup. He was apparently on the mend, and by 30 April he no longer needed his wife to nurse him, so she took a break from her duties and attended a ball at Wavertree.

On May Day, James Maybrick was back to his usual self and seemed to have made a complete recovery – until he tried to eat. The more food he consumed, the more nauseous he felt, and he would violently vomit up whatever he swallowed. Suddenly, on 3 May, he went into a full-scale relapse, and his condition started to worsen to such an alarming extent, that Florence called for Dr William Carter, an eminent Rodney Street physician. When Dr Carter arrived, he was escorted to Mr Maybrick's bedroom, where he found his patient in a very sorry state. Maybrick was writhing in agony from stomach pains, and had clearly been vomiting profusely. Dr Carter examined him and concluded that he was suffering from acute dyspepsia. The doctor assured Florence that her husband would be as right as rain in a few days.

That afternoon, Alice Yapp, the children's nurse, spotted Florence Maybrick pouring medicine from one bottle into another in a rather furtive manner. The nurse found this behaviour very suspicious, and on the following day, she decided to root through some of Mrs Maybrick's possessions. In a trunk belonging to Florence, the nurse discovered a packet labelled 'Arsenic'. This was just the proof that Nurse Yapp needed to confirm her suspicions and she rushed off to tell Mrs Matilda Briggs, an old friend of Mr Maybrick, about the find.

Then, the motive behind the misdeed was discovered, on the afternoon of 8 May, when Mrs Maybrick gave Nurse Yapp a letter to post. This letter was addressed to: 'A Brierley, Esq, 60 Huskisson Street, Liverpool'. According to Nurse Yapp, on the way to the post office, she gave the letter to Mrs Maybrick's baby daughter, Gladys, and the child dropped the letter in mud. According to the nurse, she took the letter out of its sullied envelope and placed it in a new, clean envelope that she bought at the post office.

Now, before she transferred the letter to the new envelope, Nurse Yapp admitted that she could not help noticing that Mrs Maybrick had described her husband's condition in the letter as 'sick unto death'. Considering the fact that Mr Maybrick was only supposed to be suffering from dyspepsia, the phrase 'sick unto death' struck her as rather extreme, to say the least. The prying Nurse Yapp also noticed that Mrs Maybrick had referred to Alfred Brierley as 'my own darling' in the letter. She quickly resolved not to post the letter, but to show it instead to Mrs Briggs, the housekeeper.

Mrs Briggs related her suspicions to Maybrick's brothers Edwin and Michael, and the two men set off without delay for Battlecrease House to investigate. When they arrived, Edwin showed his brother the letter that Nurse Yapp had opened. After a quick perusal, Michael denounced Mrs Maybrick as an adulteress.

The brothers then went upstairs and were both deeply shocked at the poor state of their brother. Michael visited Dr Humphrey's home that night and told him about the fly-papers in the bowl and how Nurse Yapp suspected Mrs Maybrick of poisoning her husband. Dr Humphreys, however, did not take their allegations seriously.

At 8.30pm on 11 May, James Maybrick died, surrounded by his family and friends, but Florence was not amongst them. Earlier that day, at around 11am, she had fainted from the exhaustion brought on by the long hours spent at her sick husband's bedside and was lying in a semi-conscious state on the bed in the dressing room when Mr Maybrick expired.

After the death, Nurse Yapp renewed her detective work with increased vigour and, while her mistress was still indisposed, she rummaged yet again through her possessions and discovered a brown paper parcel and a chocolate box. In the box were two bottles labelled 'Arsenic' and the words, 'Poison for cats' had also been written on the label, in red ink. The brown paper parcel contained a yellowish powder. The brothers informed a solicitor about the find, and he advised them to keep any potential evidence in a safe place, so they locked the chocolate box and the parcel in the wine cellar.

Garston Police were later notified of the death, and were also alerted to the fact that the circumstances surrounding Mr Maybrick's death were suspicious. An Inspector Baxendale soon turned up and interviewed the Maybrick brothers, Mrs Briggs, and all of the servants, before viewing James Maybrick's body. Baxendale heard of Yapp's and the servants' suspicions regarding Florence, and the next day, Michael Maybrick took the package of arsenic that Yapp had found, from the cellar, and handed it over to the inspector. That same day, Superintendent Isaac Bryning instructed his men to gather samples from the drains of Battlecrease House, in case there were traces of arsenic down there.

The post-mortem, which took place at five o'clock that afternoon, threw up lots of information which only served to strengthen the suspicions of the Maybrick brothers and Nurse Yapp. The entire lining of Maybrick's stomach was dappled with black patches, and the duodenum was scarlet and raw with severe inflammation. Dr Alexander Barron, a Professor of Pathology, and Dr Humphreys, carried out the post-mortem together, and Dr Carter took notes throughout. Maybrick's stomach was removed and placed in a jar, which was sealed then handed to Inspector Baxendale.

According to Dr Barron, Maybrick's death was due to acute inflammation of the stomach, which had been caused by an irritant poison.

***

On 14 May, Florence Maybrick was arrested, taken to the local police station in Lark Lane and then escorted to Walton Gaol. A female warder took charge of Mrs Maybrick's valuables, before leading her off to a cell in the prison's hospital.

The trial opened at St George's Hall on 31 July and lasted for seven days. The servants of Battlecrease House each supplied their own damning evidence, and so did Michael Maybrick and the various chemists who had innocently supplied Florence with her deadly supply of arsenic. All of this evidence was crowned by the expert testimony of Dr Stevenson, the Home Office toxicologist, who stated categorically that Mr Maybrick had died of arsenical poisoning. On the final day of the trial, at 3.56pm, the Clerk of Arraigns addressed the sombre jury and asked, "Have you agreed upon a verdict gentlemen?" The foreman of the jury, a Mr Wainwright, replied, "We have".

"And do you find the prisoner guilty of the murder of James Maybrick, or not guilty?"

"Guilty," intoned Mr Wainwright, triggering a wave of melancholy gasps and sighs from the gallery.

Florence trembled slightly and buried her face in her hands. The Clerk of Arraigns turned towards her and repeated the verdict and asked if she would like to address the court.

"Florence Elizabeth Maybrick, you have been found guilty of wilful murder. Have you anything to say why the court should not pronounce sentence upon you?"

Florence rose unsteadily from her seat in the dock and clutched the rail tightly to steady herself and bowed to his lordship the judge.

"My lord, everything has been against me," she began. "Although evidence has been given as to a great many circumstances in connection with Mr Brierley, much has been withheld which might have influenced the jury, had it been told. I am not guilty of this crime."

Moments later, the judge donned the black silk cap and solemnly read out the death sentence. The court was silent except for the muffled sobs and sniffles of several women in the public gallery. Utterly bereft, Florence sat alone in the dock, a pitiful figure, crying like a child.

In contrast to the relative calm inside the courtroom, when news of the verdict reached the huge crowd assembled outside on the plateau and steps of St George's Hall, their hisses could be heard along the entire length of Lime Street. Later, when several servants who had given evidence emerged from St George's Hall, a rabble-rouser in the waiting crowd wrongly identified one of them as Nurse Yapp, and the multitudes became agitated to such an extent, that seventy policemen were quickly summoned to control the dangerous overspill of people from the area. As the servants were hurriedly herded into a cab, the mob bombarded them with profanities and spat at them.

Later that day, when the judge who had sentenced Mrs Maybrick left St George's Hall under a heavy police guard, the frenzied mobs jeered him and attacked the carriage into which he was rather keenly climbing. When the carriage finally managed to escape from the thronged courtyard, a chant of "Shame! Shame!" began.

An hour later, the crowd had still not disbanded, and mounted police had to be brought in to prepare the exit route for the prison van that was to take Florence Maybrick to the gallows at Walton Gaol. Florence was escorted to the van, and as soon as the vehicle started to move through the courtyard, a tremendous deafening cheer swelled up and did not fade until the van was lost to the sight of the furious crowd.

At Walton Gaol, Florence was placed in the condemned cell to await her fate. The date of the execution was to be Monday 26 August. Long before the dreaded date, Florence had to listen to the terrifying sawing and hammering sounds, as the gallows was erected at the gaol.

But beyond the prison walls, an astounding turn of events was unfolding. A majority of the people in this country and abroad thought that the Maybrick verdict was grossly unjust, and the Home Secretary was inundated with countless petitions for a reprieve – but time was starting to run out.

Four days before the execution date, Florence was walking in Walton's prison yard, when Mr Anderson, the Governor of the gaol, called out her name as she approached him.

"Maybrick," he said, "no commutation of sentence has come down today, and I consider it is my duty to tell you to prepare for death."

Florence's reply was dignified.

"Thank you, Governor. My conscience is clear. God's will be done," she said.

That night, Florence Maybrick knelt before her bunk bed and fervently said her prayers. She then went to bed and tried to sleep. At half-past one that morning she was awakened from an uneasy sleep by the increasing cacophony of wheels trundling over the courtyard outside. It was the cab of the Queen's Messenger, who had travelled up from London bearing good news. Moments later, a key rattled in the lock of her cell door, and Florence sat up in bed, waiting anxiously to hear her fate. The Governor entered, accompanied by the Prison Chaplain and a warder.

Florence listened in dreamy disbelief as the Governor excitedly told her that she had been reprieved.

Florence's sentence was commuted to life imprisonment, and

she spent fifteen years as prisoner P29 in the gaols of Aylesbury and Woking, and did not enjoy freedom until July 1904. After her release, Florence travelled to Rouen to be reunited with her mother, the Baroness von Roques. Towards the end of August that year, Florence decided to return to America. Months after her emotional homecoming, she wrote a book about her experiences in prison, entitled *My Fifteen Lost Years*.

Florence later dropped her famous (some would say infamous) surname and replaced it with her maiden name, Chandler. She shunned all publicity and became something of an eccentric recluse. She moved to Florida, then to Illinois, before finally spending her last days in an anonymous little shack among the woodlands of Connecticut. In 1927, she made a final visit to Liverpool to attend the Grand National. On 24 November 1941, Florence was found dead in her little shack. She was seventy-eight years old.

Twisted Sisters

In 1889, Florence Maybrick achieved international notoriety as a ruthless schemer when she was found guilty of murdering her husband, James Maybrick, by arsenical poisoning. While Florence was very lucky to escape death by hanging, two sisters in Liverpool were not so fortunate after they were found guilty of ending four lives with the aid of arsenic.

In 1880, Irish widows, Catherine Flannagan and Margaret Higgins, lived at Skirving Street in Liverpool. The other occupants of the house were: Catherine's son, twenty-two-year-old John Flannagan, lodger Patrick Jennings and his sixteen-year-old daughter Margaret, another lodger named Thomas Higgins and his eight-year-old daughter Mary.

In the December of that year, consumption claimed the life of John Flannagan – or so people thought. His mother, Catherine, collected a sum of insurance in excess of seventy one pounds because of his death. Just a year after the death of John Flannagan, Margaret wed Thomas Higgins, and by November of 1882, his teenager daughter, Mary Higgins was also dead. Margaret Higgins collected twenty-two pounds insurance money on this occasion.

The neighbours of Flannagan and Higgins took the deaths of John and Mary to be coincidental. The gossiping superstitious Irish Liverpudlians in the Skirving Street area claimed deaths occurred in threes, and they were right. Within a mere two months after the death of Mary Higgins, Margaret Jennings died.

Once again, insurance money was collected. In fact, none of the deaths was due to illness at all – they were the result of murder by poisoning. On each occasion, Catherine Flannagan and Margaret Higgins had patiently waited until their victims were ill before giving them 'the send-off dose' of arsenic. This made it so much easier to obtain the necessary death certificate from the doctor for the insurance claim.

Suspicions started to get aroused in the sisters' neighbourhood, so the women though it wise to move house and they went to 105 Latimer Street. No deaths occurred there, but in September 1883, Flannagan and Higgins moved to 27 Ascot Street, where Thomas Higgins was to meet his end in October of that year as a result of their dirty work. He was insured for almost one hundred pounds and the sisters stood to gain an extra fifty pounds on a supplemental policy, but the attempt failed when the intoxicated Thomas Higgins refused to undergo the mandatory medical examination.

After the death of Thomas, his brother Patrick paid a visit to a number of insurance societies and discovered that the money had already been drawn. Patrick thought this was questionable, so he approached a physician and told him of his suspicions regarding the two sisters. The doctor and Patrick went to a coroner for advice. The police were notified and the funeral of Thomas Higgins was halted so that a post-mortem could be carried out. Margaret Higgins was subsequently arrested, and Catherine Flannagan managed to flee from the house, but was captured and taken into custody days later.

Flannagan and Higgins were charged with murder on 16 October that year when the coroner revealed that arsenic had been found in the corpse of Thomas Higgins. The three other victims were then exhumed, and traces of arsenic were found in each of the bodies. After a trial that lasted three days, the jury found Catherine Flannagan and Margaret Higgins guilty of the murders within a mere forty minutes. The sisters were sentenced to death, and were hanged at Kirkdale Gaol on 3 March 1884.

The Tragedy of Anytime Annie

There are numerous fallacies that the human race will give credence to. Most of us have heard of the 'hair of the dog' and other hangover cures, where people recovering from a night of heavy drinking imbibe alcohol, or a concoction of egg and milk, in an effort to rid their bodies of the effects of alcohol. There is of course, no known drug – not even caffeine in a black coffee – that will remove alcohol from the body. The only thing that can cure a hangover is time.

In the nineteenth century, there was a despicable fallacy about venereal disease. The widespread belief was that it could be cured by having intercourse with a virgin child. In this day and age, when thirteen-year-old school children are routinely warned about the dangers of sexually transmitted diseases, it seems inconceivable that adults were once ignorant enough to actually believe that such diseases could be cured by having sex with a virgin. However, in Victorian and Edwardian times, sex was a taboo subject and in the minds of many was regarded as solely for the purpose of producing children. Penicillin would not be accidentally discovered until the 1920s, so the main treatment for syphilis or gonorrhea was mercury, which was not only painful to take, but was also largely ineffective, and its side-effects included kidney and brain damage, impotence, anaemia and loosened teeth. Little sympathy was shown to sufferers, because Victorians viewed venereal disease, not as a medical condition, but a payback from God for immorality – the wages of sin, so to speak.

In Liverpool, like many other major cities of the world in the Victorian period, there existed a flourishing trade in pre-teen virgins – not only to cater for paedophiles from the upper reaches of society – but because these unfortunate boys and girls were seen as a safe way for a man to achieve sexual release, without the risk of contracting a venereal disease. In the early 1860s, three mentally-impaired children aged nine, seven and five years old, were repeatedly raped whilst in the care of the Liverpool Lock Hospital. The children were all seriously ill with venereal disease by the time they were approaching their tenth birthdays.

In 1861, one 'gentleman', named Alfred Ricks, developed syphilitic ulcers on his penis shortly after having intercourse with a prostitute in Kirkdale. In a desperate bid to cure himself of his condition, Ricks decided to commit an act of gross indecency with a fourteen-year-old match seller named Kate Williams. He was subsequently arrested, but proceeded to defend himself by explaining that he had only resorted to the deplorable assault in order to cure himself of his painful and disfiguring complaint. Ricks was merely fined by the court, but his innocent young victim became seriously ill with venereal disease and she later became blind.

Venereal diseases were not confined to the so-called lower classes. King Edward VII is said to have infected his wife, Queen Alexandra, with a severe strain of syphilis which manifested itself in a particularly nasty rash that gradually covered her entire body. A horrified female servant who was in attendance when the Queen divested herself of her high-collared blouse, described the pustules and scabs which completely covered the monarch's neck and extended down towards her cleavage. Edward's physician established that the King had picked up the disease in the course of his continental canoodlings.

In Liverpool, in 1871, a nine-year-old orphan named Annie Jones was with a group of ragged children eagerly waiting for a Punch and Judy Show to begin, opposite Lime Street Station. As the squeal of reed pipes and the banging of a drum heralded the imminent appearance of Mr Punch, a refined-looking gentleman accosted little Annie. The mechanism by which he persuaded the child to accompany him to a hansom cab is not known, but it was probably the promise of a florin, or some such reward.

The girl was found, distraught and sobbing uncontrollably, in the early hours of the following morning, wandering about in Islington. The poor child bore all the physical evidence of a savage sexual attack and from the garbled account which she gave to the police, it was established that Annie had been sexually assaulted by two men simultaneously. The attack had been entirely premeditated and they had plied her with food and bathed her beforehand. Annie had described the place where the assault took place as a "big house with a red carpet".

The police were powerless to act upon such a scant description of the crime scene, and the wicked perpetrators of the shocking offence were never identified or brought to justice. Not only had Annie's childhood innocence been shattered irreparably, but the girl had also contracted venereal disease from the double rape. Two years later, a man who had been appointed to become Annie's guardian was also discovered to be a paedophile. Annie recounted to the police how her custodian and a group of his friends had forced her to perform a variety of vile sexual acts upon each of them on numerous occasions. The eleven-year-old also told how her mocking abusers had even nicknamed her 'Anytime Annie'.

Such a succession of child abuse, not surprisingly, seems to have had a highly detrimental effect on Annie's mind, for she developed a deep distrust of all men and became increasingly reclusive. By 1880, she was blossoming into a pretty eighteen-year-old. She was at that age when many girls' thoughts are preoccupied with love and romance and life is yet an unfulfilled promise. She should have had everything to live for. Sadly, however, that same year, the troubled girl could no longer bear to live with her awful memories and decided to take her own life.

Lock Ah Tam

In the early hours of 2 December 1925, Lock Ah Tam, a respected member of northern England's Chinese community, shot and killed his Welsh-born wife Catherine and their two daughters, Doris and Cecilia, at their Birkenhead home. The killings were committed in a fit of rage shortly after a dinner party that had been held to celebrate the twentieth birthday of Lock Ling, Tam's son. Shortly after the triple murder, Tam lifted the receiver of his telephone and spoke to the operator in a calm and collected manner.

"I have shot my wife and children," he declared, without a

trace of emotion in his voice.

The operator listened in shocked disbelief.

"I beg your pardon, sir?" she eventually managed to stammer out.

"Please put me through to the Town Hall," Tam continued.

The operator nervously fumbled at the bank of sockets before her and instead put the Cantonese man through to Birkenhead Central Police Station. The desk sergeant picked up his pencil as he routinely did whenever the telephone rang, and he listened to Tam's low sombre voice.

"Send your folks, please. I have killed my wife and children."

The desk sergeant soon alerted his colleagues and a number of them soon turned up at Tam's home at 122 Price Street and surveyed the scene of the crime. The three bodies lay in large pools of congealed blood. Tam's son, Lock Ling, was nowhere to be found, having fled in panic from his maniacal father at the beginning of the attack. So began the inquiry into the genesis of the tragic domestic shooting.

Lock Ah Tam had been born in Canton in 1872, and in the summer of 1895, at the age of twenty-three, he travelled to England as a ship's steward, then taking up a postion at a Liverpool shipping office. Tam immediately made a favourable impression on his employers as a hardworking, jovial and honest young man, who spoke English better than most Liverpudlians. He settled down at a fine house in Birkenhead, and was soon selected to be a European representative of what was, in all except name, a Chinese seamen's trade union. Despite Tam's rise into the realms of the middle class, he remained very sympathetic to the poor, to the underdog. It was a common sight to see him stopping in the street to give half-crowns to barefooted ragamuffin children.

Lock Ah Tam's charitable deeds continued, and he was responsible for establishing a club in Liverpool where Chinese sailors could socialise and drink with friends over games of cribbage and billiards. Tam, largely at his own expense, made the club for his countrymen a reality, but unfortunately this establishment was to become the scene of a violent incident which would lead to the death of four people – including Tam himself.

One evening, in February 1918, just before the commencement of the Chinese New Year, Tam paid a visit to the new club to enjoy a glass of whisky (to which he would add two teaspoonfuls of salt) and a game of billiards. The game was in progress when a gang of drunken Russian seamen barged into the club shouting profanities and racist remarks at the Chinese members. Lock Ah Tam approached one of the troublemakers and ordered him and his friends to leave at once. One of the Russians grabbed a billiard cue and whipped it down on Tam's head. Tam slumped to the floor, with blood trickling from a long gash on the crown of his scalp. A fight broke out between the belligerent Russians and the Chinese sailors, and the police swooped on the club. Tam appeared to have recovered from the assault and accompanied the police to a nearby lodging house later that night, in order to identify the man who had hit him with the cue.

Tam was advised by a doctor not to fall asleep for a while, as he was obviously suffering from the effects of concussion. At the time it was thought that the blow to his head had done no serious damaged, but it soon became evident that he had sustained some brain injury. He began to suffer from blinding headaches and to undergo violent mood swings. His personality changed completely, and the kind, thoughtful Tam was transformed into a forgetful, short-tempered man, forever prone to pick a quarrel with anyone. His drinking habits also changed for the worse. Not only did he consume more drink, he mixed the spirits he drank, and was soon suffering from chronic alcoholism.

One evening, shortly after the fight with the Russians at the club, Tam was driven to his home in a taxi cab. After paying the driver, on a whim he invited him into the house for a drink. The taxi driver accepted the generous offer, but shortly after he entered the house, he noticed a disturbing change in his host's mood. A couple of glasses and a bottle of whisky were slammed down hard on the dining room table by Tam, who started to grit his teeth and mutter angrily to himself. The cabman, probably in an attempt to placate his new, irascible friend, made a sycophantic remark about the people of China being honest and hardworking, which sent Lock Ah Tam into a furious rage. He yelled a stream of abuse at the terrified taxi driver and ordered him to leave the house at once.

In 1924 he became bankrupt from a failed business venture, and this blow seemed to accelerate the gradual psychological deterioration of a man who had once been a pillar of the community. Catherine, his wife, loyally stood by him, despite the bankruptcy, despite the violent rages, for she knew in her heart that the cerebral injury was responsible for her husband's behavioural problems. Margaret Sing, a young woman who acted as a companion and confidante to Catherine, also lived in the house on Price Street, and often comforted her friend after the many domestic altercations. She urged her to leave her violent husband on numerous occasions, but Catherine insisted that she was still in love with Tam and would not consider leaving him.

On the last day of November, 1925, Lock Ah Tam's son, Lock Ling, turned twenty. Ling had only recently returned from China, where he had just spent nine years completing his schooling. Tam held a dinner party to celebrate his son's birthday and homecoming. The party passed without incident, but later that night, shortly after the family had retired to their beds, Lock Ling was awakened by the alarming sounds of a fight coming from his parent's bedroom. He immediately jumped out of bed and, with his sisters, who had also been awakened by the fighting, he barged into his mother and father's room. Ling accused his father of being a wife-beater, and warned him that he would take his mother next door to spend the night with Mr and Mrs Chin if he continued to act like a brute. Tam was furious at this intervention and claimed that he had never laid a finger on his wife. All the same, Ling and his sisters surrounded their terrified mother and ushered her into the sitting room on the same floor.

Ling pleaded for her to go with him to the safety of the Chins' home next door, because he feared that his father had become dangerously unstable. Catherine refused to accompany him and so did her daughters, Doris and Cecilia. Lock Ling tearfully decided that he could not sleep under the same roof as his deranged father, and so, in a huff, he went to spend the night with his neighbours. His mother and sisters, meanwhile, remained barricaded in the sitting room for the rest of the night.

The next morning, Tam called out for Margaret Sing – Catherine's friend – from his bedroom. Margaret cautiously responded to the master of the house and Lock Ah Tam came out onto the landing and told her to bring his boots. Margaret dutifully brought him the boots and Tam took them from her, before abruptly telling her to get dressed.

Margaret returned to her room, hastily put on her coat and then went back to Tam's bedroom. She did not knock on the door, which was ajar, but instead peeped curiously into the room. What she saw sent her running in terror to Catherine. Tam had been staring in the bedroom mirror, and his face had been twisted in a grotesque mask of evil hatred. What was even more frightening was that Tam held a revolver in his shaking hand.

Margaret fled along the landing and urgently knocked on the

sitting room door and Doris let her in. After bolting the door behind her, she breathlessly told the three women what she had just witnessed. Moments later, the sitting room door was almost hammered off its hinges as Tam pounded upon it and screamed to be let in. The hammering lasted for a few minutes, then all became quiet. The women strained their ears and listened to Tam's faint footsteps as he returned to his room.

When they felt that it was safe to do so, the four women hurried away from the sitting room and crept down the stairs. They hid in the kitchen, where Lock Ling was standing with the next door neighbour Mrs Chin. Ling once again tried his utmost to persuade his mother to go next door for her own safety, but once more she refused. Margaret Sing, Doris and Cecilia took their lead from Catherine and also decided to stay put in the house for the time being. They all hoped that Lock Ah Tam's 'fit' would soon pass. Lock Ling had a more realistic view of the situation, and he rushed out of the house in search of a policeman.

"Let's go to the scullery," Margaret Sing suggested, and she collected some crockery and left the kitchen, perhaps intending to make tea for the long hours ahead.

The other women, including Mrs Chin, followed Margaret into the scullery, which was one of the smallest rooms in the house. There was barely enough elbow room for the five women and Margaret had to stand behind the wide-open door with Mrs Chin and Doris. Cecilia was huddled into a space next to the cast iron stove and her mother stood squarely in the doorframe.

All at once there was a loud bang, and Catherine's whole body shook. She glanced in horror at her daughter, Doris, then fell to the stone floor. There was a moment of frozen silence when time seemed to stand still. Before anyone could make a move, there was a second loud report, and this time Cecilia's eye's first widened and then rolled, and the girl fell down dead. Her eyes gazed lifelessly at the ceiling. A shiny metal tube slid ominously into view around the doorframe – the barrel of Lock Ah Tam's revolver. His hand raised the gun and he fired it once more, this time blasting Doris, who was trying to scream from a throat closed up with terror. She slumped to her knees and looked up at Mrs Chin. The girl's mouth seemed to be saying, "Why?"

Doris fell forward and her head hit the stone floor with a sickening thump. Margaret Sing was so distraught that she lost control of her bladder as she awaited her turn to die, while Mrs Chin was more angry than afraid. Tam seemed oblivious to the two living women's presence, and they watched as he foamed at the mouth, trembling as he surveyed the bodies of his family on the floor. Without saying a word, he then turned around and walked to the telephone to alert the police to the triple murder.

The trial of Lock Ah Tam opened on 5 February 1926, before Mr Justice MacKinnon. Tam was defended by Sir Edward Marshall Hall, who argued that his client had been in a state of 'unconscious automatism', brought on by an epileptic fit, and had therefore been in a state of insanity when he committed the senseless murders.

The jury, however, was not convinced by this explanation, and took a mere twelve minutes to reach a verdict of guilty. The court was filled with many of Tam's friends, many of whom cried openly when the judge passed the sentence of death. Lock Ah Tam remained calm and collected throughout the reading of the sentence and even smiled as the judge donned the black cap.

Lock Ah Tam was executed by hangmen, William Willis and Henry Pollard, at Walton Prison on 23 March of that same year.

The Resurrection Men

The following gruesome incident unfolded many years ago, just across the road from the Cambridge pub, in Mulberry Street. Shortly before eleven o'clock one foggy night in October 1826, an eleven-year-old orphan named Jim Buckles, of Egypt Street, pounded on the door of a lodging house on the corner of Mulberry Street. The keeper of the house, a large stocky man named John McAllister, went to the door with a lantern in his hand, wondering who was calling at such a late hour. "Who's there?" he shouted, but no reply came. Curiosity got the better of him, and he put down the lantern and brought the poker from his grate.

When McAllister opened the door, little Jim Buckles flew past him and hid under a table, where he trembled and uttered an odd, subdued moan. Outside in the fog, three ghostly shadows came forward, then halted. Moments later they melted back into the night vapours like spectres. The landlord sensed that evil was afoot upon this fog-shrouded night, and he closed the door, bolted it, then turned his attention to the frightened boy.

McAllister bent down slowly and peeped under the table. He vaguely recognised the orphan from the home for destitute children in the area, but he did not yet know that the child was mute, unable to speak.

"What's your game?" McAllister asked, and he thrust the lantern at the child under the table, who was making noises, trying desperately to speak. His eyes told the landlord that he was terrified.

When McAllister eventually realised that the boy could not talk, he calmed him down and handed him his quill. The boy was surprisingly good at sketching, and he scratched the nib across the torn-out page of an old ledger. What he drew was very curious. He sketched the outlines of four open coffins, surrounded by what looked like gravestones. Then he drew men with scarves around their faces. They held spades and a lantern. Little Jimmy drew what clearly resembled bodies in shrouds lying about.

This could obviously mean only one thing: grave robbers, body snatchers, or 'Resurrection Men' as they were then called. Perhaps Jimmy had caught them red handed as they were digging up corpses, McAllister speculated, since the orphans' home lay in close proximity to the cemetery. Then McAllister recalled seeing the faint shadows in the fog earlier. Had they been the Resurrection Men in pursuit of Jimmy?

Deciding that the boy's life was probably in danger, McAllister let him stay in a tiny spare room under the eaves of the lodging house, and the next day the landlord went to the police, but they refused to take the boy's sketches seriously. Amazingly, no one was sent to Mulberry Street cemetery to see if any of the graves had been disturbed. One of the detectives decided that Jim Buckles was just an orphan trying to worm his way into McAllister's house and he warned the landlord to be wary of him. McAllister was disgusted and disappointed by the detective's reaction.

On the following night, an oppressive October fog crept in from the Mersey and blanketed the streets. McAllister was letting out his two cats when he caught sight of a man in a long, black coat throttling a boy – it was young Jimmy. McAllister shouted for him to stop and the stranger threw the boy down and dashed off, vanishing into the murky fog. The boy was badly shaken up by his ordeal and was left with severe bruising on his neck, but he recovered, and once again McAllister took pity on him and put him up at the lodging house. The boy could throw no light on the motivation for the attack. He had been returning from an errand which he had run for a woman just a street away, when the strange man in black had seized him.

That same night, three large wooden casks were loaded onto a ship, the *Latona*. The ship was berthed at George's Dock passage near the Pier Head, bound to sail for Leith in Scotland in the morning. Three casks on board started to give off an appalling, putrid smell. The suspicious sailors on the *Latona* could stand the strong stench no longer and prised open the casks; they discovered eleven bodies concealed in them. The naked bodies of the eleven men, women and children were piled on top of each other and packed in salt.

The police soon traced the man who had carted the casks to the *Latona*, who told them that a Scottish man had paid him two shillings to transport them from a cellar at 8 Hope Street. The police arrived at the Hope Street address, where a Reverend McGowan refused to admit them onto the premises. The Reverend was warned that he was impeding an investigation and could be imprisoned for such an obstruction of police procedure. The cleric looked very worried by something, and he suddenly broke down and gave a garbled story about renting his cellar to a Mr Henderson, a Scot who had claimed to be a fish oil exporter. At this, the policemen pushed the Reverend McGowan aside and descended the steps to the cellar.

Down in the cellar the hard-boiled policemen felt faint as they came upon twenty-two corpses strewn haphazardly about the floor. Mass murder was initially suspected, but each corpse bore the telltale scars of a post-mortem examination. In other words, the corpses had been disinterred from the local graveyard in Mulberry Street.

The mysterious Mr Henderson managed to evade capture, but his lackeys did not, and they were identified by little Jimmy Buckles, who had witnessed them digging up the graves. Each of the Resurrection Men was given twelve months hard labour, after paying a hefty fine. Each corpse would have netted fifteen pounds had the grave-robbing scheme worked. They would have received the money from the Scottish medical schools, in return for the corpses, which would have been used for dissection by medical students studying human anatomy.

The Demon Drink

Not surprisingly, 'the demon drink' has been at the root of many a murder in the North West, just as elsewhere, and the following are just a few examples.

Thomas Corrigan murdered his mother on 1 November 1873, following a prolonged drinking spree. Returning home after drinking heavily for hours, he assaulted several neighbours and members of his family, before finally striking and jumping on his mother and brutally killing her.

After the jury returned a verdict of 'guilty of murder' at his trial, the judge remarked on the enormity of the crime. In his opinion, it was made worse by the fact that Corrigan had killed someone he was 'bound to love and cherish'.

The execution, at Kirkdale Gaol, was carried out by Mr Anderson, who replaced Calcraft, following the mistakes he had made during the hanging of James O'Connor.

***

William Baker, the argumentative manager of the Railway Vaults, in Williamson Square, spent 10 July 1875 drinking with three friends in a selection of the many tough pubs along Scotland Road. In the early hours of the following morning, Baker and his friends were refused entry into an illegal drinking hole in Back Bridport Street. A man named Charles Langan, who was leaving the illicit club, rubbed salt into Baker's wounds by making jibes about his appearance and his antics at being turned away from the underworld establishment.

Langan followed the irate publican to London Road, where a fierce altercation took place. Baker suddenly produced a revolver and swore at Langan, before blasting him at point blank range. The bullet entered his chest and exited through his back. Langan slumped to the pavement with a look of horrified amazement on his face. He poked his fingertip into the bullet hole in his chest, perhaps in shock, or maybe in a vain attempt to stem the steady trickle of his life's blood. He was subsequently pronounced dead on arrival at the nearby Royal Infirmary.

The ensuing trial lasted only a single day. Baker was found guilty of murder, and a 'recommendation of mercy' was made by the jury, but not upheld by the judge, and Baker too was hanged at Kirkdale Gaol.

***

In 1858, an habitual drunkard named Jane Parker gave birth to a son at Preston. Only hours after the birth she commenced a tour of her local tavern showing off the new-born babe, during the so-called 'wetting the baby's head' ceremony. Gin and water were ceremoniously dabbed on the infant's head, and Jane was plied with far too many drinks by the regulars.

In a grossly intoxicated state, the girl began a surreal argument with one of the regulars propping up the bar, who maintained that a newly born baby could survive in a wooden box for two days without food and water. In her befuddled state, Jane was determined to prove him wrong, and she staggered round to a furniture shop in the area to purchase a small box. With careless abandon she placed her baby boy in this box, and paid a labourer three pence to transport it to the railway station. The note on the box began, 'Mrs Melville ...' followed by a Liverpool address.

It is not difficult to imagine the horror that Mrs Melville of Liverpool experienced when she opened that parcel. The baby boy inside was still barely alive, but looked pinched and blue with cold and hunger. Mrs Melville desperately tried to revive the little mite by warming him in front of the fire, but to no avail. The child was then taken to the Northern Dispensary Hospital, where he was pronounced dead on arrival.

Why Jane Parker chose Mrs Melville's address is a mystery. However, the police soon traced the parcel back to the baby's wicked mother, and when the officers of the law moved in on her, Parker seized a bottle of laudanum and tried to gulp it down, but her overdose attempt was thwarted by the lightning reflexes of one of the policemen, who stormed into her quarters and managed to swipe the bottle out of her hand.

Jane Parker was arrested and later found guilty of manslaughter. The six months with hard labour which she was given by the court hardly seems a sufficient punishment for so heinous a crime.

Impossible Dilemma

Despite having no medical qualifications, Alfred Heap chose to call himself a surgeon. In fact, all he did was sell simple herbal remedies and homemade concoctions from his shop. This shop was actually nothing more than an elaborate front for Heap's main source of income, his private (and illegal) abortion service.

In the Spring of 1875, confectioner, Mary McKivett, found herself pregnant – to her uncle. In those times being an unmarried mother would be an unbearable stigma in itself, but what would people say if they found out that a niece had slept with her own uncle and had borne his child as a result? Her reputation and future life would be ruined. Mary examined her dilemma from every angle and concluded that there was only one course of action open to her.

Like everyone else in the neighbourhood, she was well aware of the true nature of Heap's business and so, like so many desperate women before her, she reluctantly visited his shop. There she purchased a solution which would, Heap assured her, cause her to miscarry, apparently with no ill effects.

Mary McKivett felt that she had no alternative, and whilst she did not altogether trust Heap, she swallowed the mixture according to his instructions as soon as she arrived home. Not only did the drug not have the required effect, the poor woman subsequently died from the effects of Heap's concoction. It was not long before the so-called surgeon was arrested by the detectives investigating the girl's suspicious death.

Heap was sent to the assizes to be tried for murder and he was found guilty – even though the jury made a recommendation of mercy. This was not granted, due to a previous conviction for carrying out an illegal abortion, for which he received a sentence of five years imprisonment.

Heap was hanged at Kirkdale Gaol.

The Duel At Knotts Hole

In the now redundant church of St James, Toxteth, on the north wall under the gallery, there is a memorial tablet bearing the following inscription:

Sacred to the Memory of
EDWARD GRAYSON of Liverpool
Shipwright
An Honest Man, an Affectionate Relative and a Sincere Friend
Whose zeal in the defence of insulted Innocence caused him to fall
a Sacrifice to the Law of false Honour, Whereby the injured are unhappily
compelled to expose themselves to Destruction at the call of the aggressor.
Died March 4th 1804

The inscription refers to a scandal which affected some of the most respected Liverpool families and resulted in tragic consequences. The sequence of events started in October 1802, with the announcement of the engagement of William Sparling and Ann Renshaw. Sparling belonged to a very wealthy Liverpool family. His father, John Sparling, had amassed a huge fortune as a West Indian trader, and had been Mayor of Liverpool in 1790. He had died in 1800.

William Sparling, who in 1802 was twenty-five years old, had inherited his father's fortune, a splendid mansion in Everton called St Domingo and an extensive estate at Petton, near Ellesmere in Shropshire. He had been educated at Eton and Oriel College, Oxford and then commissioned into the 10th Hussars, a fashionable regiment nominally commanded by the Prince Regent. However, he had recently resigned his commission.

Miss Ann Renshaw, then aged thirty-two, seven years his

senior, was the daughter of Oxford-educated, Reverend Samuel Renshaw, one of Liverpool's two Rectors since 1794 and the officiating clergyman at St Peter's, Church Street. His wife was born Sarah Grayson, sister of Edward Grayson. William Sparling, Samuel Renshaw and Edward Grayson were all proprietors of the Athenaeum, a gentlemen's club in Liverpool which still exists today.

Sometime in November 1802, William Sparling received an anonymous letter while he was at his country estate at Petton, which stated that his proposed wedding to Ann Renshaw would be a tremendous mistake. She was accused of vulgarity and of only marrying Sparling for his money. Her anonymous accuser also insinuated that a previous admirer had 'enjoyed her favours to the full'. For good measure, the author claimed that the Renshaw family was noted for its inherited insanity.

Sparling later testified that he knew full well that some of the accusations in the letter were false, but there were others that he could not be sure about, which, if they were true, would afford an insurmountable objection to the marriage. He did not specify which particulars he knew to be false. After some reflection, he asked his mother to acquaint Miss Renshaw with the contents of the letter. Sparling met Samuel Renshaw at his Bold Street home on 8 December 1802, agreeing that further enquiries should be made.

By this time, however, Mrs Sparling had already stated her strong objections to the marriage and had expressed these most decisively to her son. Accordingly, that same day, 8 December, Sparling wrote to Renshaw, explaining his mother's oppositions.

'You cannot be surprised at her opposition, or my approval of it ... the opposition of my friends ought to have weight in an affair of such importance ... Had I known the circumstances, I should certainly have acted differently – it is some consolation that my acquaintance has been of short duration. The decided objection of all my relatives and friends causes me to be thus explicit.'

Not surprisingly, this drew from Samuel Renshaw a letter of magisterial rebuke; he characterised Sparling as a man armed with apathy, bearing in his breast a heart buttoned up in steel, and to be connected with such a 'cool, abandoned, determined villain', would contaminate the Renshaw family.

There is no evidence of where Sparling spent the next two months, but it is probable that he went to stay at Petton. But in March 1803 he was able to go to France; the Napoleonic War had been halted by the Treaty of Amiens and many British travellers were taking advantage of the ensuing peace to visit the continent. This interlude of peace was brief and, by June 1803, the war had recommenced and he was forced to return to England, this time staying in London.

As was to be expected, Sparling's reputation in Liverpool was badly damaged. In December 1802, before his departure for France, his friend, Edward Brooks, a Customs Official and Major in the Militia, travelled with Edward Grayson, Ann Renshaw's uncle, to a dinner in Wavertree, in Grayson's gig. Brooks asked him whether a day had been fixed for the marriage of his niece, Ann Renshaw, with William Sparling. Grayson informed him that Sparling had withdrawn from the engagement following the receipt of a horrible, anonymous letter and expressed his opinion of Sparling as an infamous villain.

During the next two weeks, Brooks saw Grayson several times at the Athenaeum and other places, each time publicly abusing Sparling and threatening chastisement and also complaining that he was avoiding him. Sparling probably left England in March 1803, hoping that by lying low in France for a while, the undoubted hostility towards him in Liverpool society would be dispelled. But, when the hostilities resumed, he was forced to give up his plan and take up lodgings in London, where, in September, he was visited by both Edward Brooks and another Liverpool man, Ralph Benson, also a proprietor of the Athenaeum.

Benson told Sparling that he was wretched at hearing of Grayson's continued hostility. He indignantly claimed that he had been wrongly called a coward and a villain. Benson argued that he had contributed to his own situation by keeping his friends ignorant of such facts as would refute the damaging reports. Soon after this, Brooks visited Sparling and found him agitated and depressed. Sparling told him that he intended to return to Liverpool to clear his character.

From Webbs Hotel, Covent Garden, Sparling wrote the first of three letters to Edward Grayson, which would mark decisive stages in the quarrel and would also form a critical part of the evidence at his subsequent trial for murder.

That first letter stated briefly that Grayson had asserted that: 'he did not know where to find me. This is false, you know where to find me. You will receive this by 21st September, I insist you answer by return of post to reach me on 23rd September, when I propose leaving London. By Monday, 26th September, I shall be able to attend you at any place in the neighbourhood of Liverpool that you may think proper to appoint.'

The contents of this letter enabled Sergeant Cockell, the Attorney General for Lancaster, to make the salient point at the trial, that by inviting Grayson to appoint a meeting place, Sparling was endeavouring to make him the challenger and not the acceptor of the challenge.

By 1 October 1803, Sparling was at his country house at Petton. He wrote again to Grayson, giving Major Brooks as his authority for reporting the words about chastisement. Sparling conceded that Grayson, as a family man, could seek delay in bringing matters to a serious conclusion, stating that he would await the summons at Petton and referring Grayson to Captain Samuel Colquitt as a trusted friend.

The reference to Grayson as a family man brings us to the other principal in this affair: Edward Grayson. As we have seen already, he was brother-in-law to Samuel Renshaw and uncle of Ann Renshaw. Well-liked and respectable, he was then aged forty-six and was responsible for a profitable ship building and repair business, as well as a timber yard and saw mill on a site close to Salthouse Dock. A proprietor of the Athenaeum, a description has survived of him as a sincere and charitable man.

One of Grayson's closest friends was Dr John McCartney, whose practice and dispensary were in Duke Street. McCartney was to act eventually as Grayson's second and he took the prudent step, immediately after the duel, of lodging a statement of the facts, as known by him, at the Athenaeum. He recorded that he had, on coming to Liverpool fourteen years earlier, been befriended by Grayson. At a time when his hospitality and good offices could be of real use to a young man beginning the exercise of a laborious and arduous profession, McCartney claimed, 'I experienced from him many acts of kindness'.

It seems that when the letter of 19 September arrived at Grayson's house at 125 St James Street, he had a presentiment of disaster because, on 28 September of that same year, Grayson signed his last will and testament and appointed three executors in the presence of his solicitor and his clerk. The bulk of the estate was represented by the timber yard and offices at Salthouse Dock and it was provided that these should be sold to provide a fund for the benefit of Grayson's five children, who were aged between thirteen and twenty. Surprisingly, there was no Mrs Grayson. All these children had been born to Sarah Jackson, now Sarah Wilson, and she was provided with a legacy of thirty guineas annually for life. She had probably married Wilson quite recently. The 1801 census shows two males and one female living at 125 St James Street – Grayson, Sarah and the younger boy, Edward, then aged ten.

In the first week of October 1803, Dr McCartney, visiting a friend who lived a few miles away from Liverpool, found that another guest was his friend, Edward Grayson. Contrary to his usual demeanour, Grayson seemed to be decidedly out of spirits. Talking privately after dinner, McCartney commented on his friend's apparent melancholy and, thinking Grayson was requiring medical counsel, urged him to disclose the reason for his distress. Grayson explained about Sparling's letter and McCartney was immediately apprehensive, as he was well aware of Grayson's opinion of Sparling's conduct regarding his niece. He was astonished to hear that he had received a direct challenge from Sparling, in terms which questioned his truthfulness.

McCartney promised to reflect on the best course of action and went away to read the letters which had passed between the two men. He became deeply concerned by the possibility of serious consequences and visited Grayson the next day. He proposed that each party appoint a friend to act for him by direct conversations and correspondence. He volunteered to act for Grayson and, as the name of Captain Colquitt RR had been mentioned by Sparling, it was soon agreed that McCartney and Colquitt would seek to bring the quarrel to a peaceful conclusion.

McCartney was optimistic, he knew Colquitt personally and considered him to be a gallant and honourable man. The two met during the middle of October and Colquitt greeted McCartney in a calm, welcoming manner, saying, "Doctor, we must put an end to this business". McCartney showed him Sparling's first letter and Colquitt concluded that Sparling had acted in a precipitate manner. He was also shown a letter from Grayson which contained the reason for his seeking a delay in giving Sparling satisfaction. It appeared that he had a lease from the Corporation for his yard and buildings at Salthouse Dock for three lives, one of them being his own. The Corporation would not change lives so far advanced as Grayson's and so Grayson had offered to sell the premises at a fair valuation. Captain Colquitt admitted to McCartney that there were sound reasons for delay and he would write to Sparling to that effect.

McCartney was fully aware of the need for skilled negotiations. He could not fail to be conscious of Grayson's state of mind when the latter wrote to him on the 12 October 1803, thanking him for taking his part. Grayson had asserted that, 'every respectable inhabitant of the town acquainted with the outline of W Sparling's conduct to my niece, unanimously join in execrating the wretch who can so deliberately act so diabolical a part.'

Grayson continued that Sparling had gained an ascendancy over Ann Renshaw, she had promised to marry him and he had declared that his mother highly approved his choice. Further, he had talked about the tour they would take as a honeymoon and then had produced the notorious anonymous letter which any man of honour would have thrown into the fire.

Grayson was convinced from the postmark on the letter and from enquiries of the Postmaster, that Sparling had been in possession of the anonymous letter before leaving Liverpool for Petton and before returning and renewing his address to Ann Renshaw. Grayson concluded this long and heartfelt letter to McCartney by writing: 'Good friend, are we not embarked on a noble cause, I never thought myself a coward, I seek not the quarrel but accept the boasted challenge as an honest man – if I fall, never did man die in a more just, virtuous and honourable cause.'

Grayson's wrath was understandable, Sparling's letter of 9 October 1803 contained the following remarks, 'I will not explain my conduct to you, or Dr McCartney, but briefly remark that female honour, virtue and innocence have nothing to do with the point in question. Those qualities of Miss A Renshaw remain as I found them', which the Renshaws would have found contemptible.

McCartney was right to be alarmed at the prospect of the two principals exchanging letters and inflaming each others' temper, because Grayson, on 17 October 1803, had replied to Sparling's recent letter thus, 'that you did leave my niece's virtue and honour as you found them is as true as God reigns above, but did you, Sir, leave her peace of mind as calm and undisturbed as when you found it, the bare reflection of which, if you ever reflect at all, must freeze your blood and harrow up your very soul, particularly when, in the presence of Mr Renshaw, Mr Ellames and Mr Bolden, you declared you firmly believed the infernal anonymous letter was a wicked fabrication.'

The matter rested for a time, but Dr McCartney's hopes that passions would be calmed by the passage of time were to be proved illusory. Early in the New Year, Sparling, then at Bath, wrote to Captain Colquitt that sufficient time had been allowed for Grayson to settle this most intricate affair and he would now insist upon an immediate termination of the matter. McCartney and Colquitt held further meetings, both men becoming increasingly anxious, and when Sparling returned to Liverpool he attended a large party where Dr McCartney was mortified to hear him declare that he had returned to fight Mr Grayson.

Yet matters still did not come to a head. On the 23 January 1804, Grayson wrote a long and passionate letter to McCartney in which he reaffirmed his standpoint:

'No matter how either myself or family may suffer, I am ready to go out at an hour's notice and accept the boasted challenge. I beseech you with all the Friendship I bear you, to inform Captain Colquitt I am ready at a moment's warning and with a full reliance on my God that I shall, on the occasion, act like a true Christian and a Man of Honour.' He concluded by asking McCartney to 'keep the letter safe by you. I am writing by candlelight and my eyes are very weak that I do not attempt a copy.'

A further month passed, Sparling being absent from Liverpool for some days, but, on the 23 February 1804, when Dr McCartney returned to his house in Duke Street, he found Colquitt waiting for him. He explained that Sparling was back in Liverpool and was insisting on a duel within twenty-four hours.

McCartney and Colquitt each consulted their principals further and met later in the day, as McCartney put it: 'to explain the unfortunate business in such a manner as to prevent a meeting'. McCartney argued that words spoken at such a distance of time, when, as he said the whole town joined in an outcry against Sparling, was unreasonable. He also noted that at all times Captain Colquitt was temperate and willing to conciliate. The two men agreed to meet again at five o'clock at Duke Street, when McCartney was given Sparling's final ultimatum. He demanded that Grayson withdraw the offending words and express his regret at their use, or he must meet him the next day. Failing these alternatives, he must expect his name to be posted in the Athenaeum. This was only an empty threat as he had no authority at the Athenaeum and the President, William Roscoe, would be the last man to give any endorsement to duelling.

Within a short time, McCartney conveyed the alternatives to Grayson, who immediately saw the impossibility of complying. Sadly, McCartney then set off to the Royal Hotel in Lord Street to meet Grayson, who had gone off to borrow some pistols. Colquitt, McCartney and Grayson then agreed that the meeting should take place the next day, Sunday 26 February at 7am, at Knotts Hole, a secluded area near the river, two or three fields away from the Park Chapel, now known as the Ancient Chapel of Toxteth on Park Road.

It was agreed that McCartney should call upon Henry Parke, an eminent Liverpool surgeon, early the next morning, pretending that he wished him to visit a patient who lived near the Park Chapel. Patrick Dignan was Grayson's manservant, who, because he was a married man, Grayson allowed to sleep at his own lodgings, contrary to normal practice. At 11.30pm on 25 February, Gregson called at Dignan's lodgings and directed him to come to his house in St James' Street at 6am the next morning. Dignan complied but was fifteen minutes late, which annoyed Grayson and they set off on foot in stony silence to the Park Chapel, a distance of about a mile. By the time they arrived, two coaches were already there and stepping out of one of them was Dr McCartney. He greeted Grayson, who was still fretting about being late – it was about 6.45am. Dignan noticed Parke still sitting in the coach and Grayson asked if he could sit with him, the morning being so cold.

McCartney explained later that when he had arrived with Parke, the latter had then understood the nature of his excursion and refused to leave the coach, declaring that, had he realised what was intended, he would have informed the magistrates. It may well be that McCartney regretted for many years to come that he did not allow a slight hint of what was to come to escape his earlier conversation with Parke.

Simon Bozzon, a post-chaise driver, testified that at six o'clock that Sunday morning, he had collected Captain Colquitt and Sparling from the Royal Hotel and had driven them to the Park Chapel. As they left the chaise, instructing Bozzon to await their return, he noticed that Colquitt was carrying a small box. The pair then passed out of sight down a path through the fields, but a little while later Bozzon heard the report of a pistol shot. He stated that McCartney and Parke then returned by coach and, almost at the same time, returned Grayson and his servant. Grayson was shaking his head and looking at his watch, complaining that his servant had caused him to be half an hour late.

Grayson and McCartney then made their way down a footpath leading to what McCartney described as a valley, some one or two fields away from the road. This location was referred to by several of the witnesses at the trial as the Dingle, sometimes known as Knotts Hole.

Sparling and Colquitt were waiting for them and McCartney introduced Grayson to Sparling, the two never having met before that day. There was a brief discussion of the distance to be measured between the two duellists, Sparling wanting ten paces, but McCartney insisted on twelve. The seconds measured the ground but, upon comparing the pistols, McCartney was astonished to find that Grayson's pistols, borrowed by him the day before, were rusty. McCartney asked Colquitt for the loan of one of his pistols. There was a moment of macabre farce when Colquitt and Sparling showed Grayson how the pistol should be cocked.

The two principals took up their positions, Colquitt, at McCartney's request, giving the word of command. The two shots were fired almost instantaneously, Sparling's shot hitting Grayson on the upper right thigh. Sparling and Colquitt hurried away, promising to send Parke the surgeon, leaving Grayson bleeding profusely, supported by McCartney and another man who had appeared on the scene, identified later as the surgeon of Colquitt's ship, *Princess*. Parke arrived and Grayson was lifted into McCartney's coach and driven home, after first asking Patrick Dignan to bring his children to the house.

Parke attended Grayson for the next seven days, hoping that he would recover, but the ball could not be extracted from his thigh whicht had become infected. Delirium set in and on the following Sunday, 4 March 1804, Edward Grayson died. After the Wednesday, he had been aware of his approaching death and generously pronounced his forgiveness of Sparling, asking that his friends should not prosecute him after his death. Sparling and Colquitt, had driven back to Liverpool, calling first at the home of Ralph Benson and then at George Stavert's, Sparling's family doctor.

We are given a vivid glimpse of that Sunday morning by Benson, who testified to hearing a violent banging on the door of his house in Duke Street. From by the banister he heard his servant cry out that a man had called to say that Sparling 'has walked out and is very well'.

Stavert later testified that Sparling was in great agitation and it was some time before he could speak. He eventually managed to stammer out that he had put a ball into Grayson and hoped the injury was not dangerous. Mr Grayson had made so much noise that he concluded that the wound could not be of much consequence. He wanted Stavert to visit his mother to tell her that he was unhurt. Sparling and Colquitt were then driven to the parade strip and went on board *HMS Princess*. On the day that Grayson died, a coroner's jury was convened to hear evidence about the duel, finding that Sparling and Colquitt did murder Edward Grayson. Samuel Renshaw and Peter Ellames placed a notice in the main Liverpool newspapers, stating that Sparling and Colquitt were believed to be concealed on the frigate *Princess* , and anyone knowingly concealing them would be an accessory and guilty of felony.

Sparling and Colquitt then surrendered to the magistrates and were put on trial for murder at Lancaster Assizes on 4 April 1804, just four weeks after Grayson's death. The prosecution, led by Mr Sergeant Cockell, the Attorney General, explained to the jury that when a duel immediately followed a sudden quarrel, a fatal result could be regarded as manslaughter, but, as he put it, "if reason has time to resume her function", then the law holds a fatal result to be murder. The Attorney General went through all the steps of the quarrel, arguing that Sparling's conduct was evidence of "persevering malice, hatred and malignity". He said that if Grayson had died by Sparling's shot, and the shot had been deliberate, then both he and Colquitt were guilty of murder and he demanded that verdict from the jury.

There was, of course, no real dispute about the facts. The evidence of the various witnesses was not seriously challenged by the defence. So the team of five barristers, led by Mr Park, relied on two different lines of approach.

Firstly, they attempted to soften some of the worst evidence against Sparling. Dr McCartney was compelled to agree that Sparling had never demanded an apology from Grayson in person – only a private acknowledgement retracting his original comments was required. But McCartney riposted by asserting that Grayson could not honourably agree to this, and no doubt everyone had realised that the apology might well be private but the news of it would be public knowledge very quickly. Edward Byrne was called by the defence and he testified that at the Athenaeum, one January evening, he had seen and heard Edward Grayson saying to one proprietor, "you will probably see Sparling and you will recollect that I say he is a damned rascal".

The other line of defence relied on portraying Sparling as a mild gentle character, not at all disposed to quarrel and, in pursuit of that, Sparling's evidence was read for him by Park, having first pleaded weakness of voice. The statement was very probably written for him by one of the defence team. It added nothing to the account of the facts of the case, but again sought to soften the effect.

Sparling complained that a malignant and vindictive person had sought to blacken his character and claimed that even the

Pulpit had been profaned, no doubt with Samuel Renshaw in mind. He continued to assert his regard for Ann Renshaw and his desire that Grayson should admit that the insulting expression had escaped him in the heat of the moment. He denied the rumoured suggestion that he had been practising pistol shots before Grayson arrived, in spite of Simon Bozzon's statement claiming so.

The defence then called a good number of witnesses who testified to Sparling's character. Perhaps the most surprising witness for the defence was Reverend Jonathan Brooks, who would succeed Samuel Renshaw as Rector of Liverpool, and then was a minister at St George's Church.

The Attorney General had foreseen this line of defence in his opening address, when he cautioned the jury: "Gentlemen, although these two prisoners are men of rank and fortune, I am quite sure you will deal with their cases as you have done with the cases of other prisoners before you, unattended by the aid of fortunes, solitary and forlorn. The law of England knows no distinction of persons, the highest subject is not beyond its reach, the lowest is not beneath its protection."

The judge, Sir Alan Chambre, some of whose interventions in the proceedings had been rather inept, summed up. He repeated what the Attorney General had said about the law on duelling. He pointed out that the Renshaw family could have taken legal action against Sparling if he had broken his promise of marriage, so it was not justifiable of Grayson to use the language he did. This was true, but the same applied to Sparling; it was he who had forced the issue. The judge allowed that no provocation by Grayson could be considered as an extenuation of the offence of duelling. He then re-capitulated all the evidence of the witnesses who had testified to the good character of both defendants, praising the characters of both men.

He concluded by putting the matter thus: "If you are of the

opinion that Mr Sparling did commit the act which deprived Mr Grayson of his life, coolly and deliberately, Captain Colquitt aiding and abetting, in that case you must find them guilty. If you are dissatisfied with this, as I heartily wish you may, you may be able to observe any circumstances in the case which will warrant you to think that they are not guilty, in that case you will acquit them of the offence." He also reiterated that it did appear that Mr Sparling, on his return, showed an anxious desire that all due care should be taken of Mr Grayson.

The jury then retired and returned after twenty minutes with a verdict of 'not guilty'. Perhaps their minds had been fastened upon a letter of support for the prisoners from no less a person than the Prince Regent.

There was considerable anger in Liverpool at the verdict. The only juror summoned to the panel from the city was from Toxteth Park and he was challenged by the defence and dismissed. All the jurors were from the Manchester and Bolton areas. The obituary for Grayson in *Billinges Advertiser* was characteristic of the general view: 'Society has rarely lost a more agreeable companion, kindred a more affectionate relative, or intimates a steadier friend. He was mainly generous and sincere, kind and charitable to all who wanted assistance. He possessed a superior talent of wit and humour and successfully turned the laugh on vanity and pride, but never debased it by calumny or ill nature.'

William Sparling never returned to Liverpool. His fine house, Saint Domingo, was put up for sale and for the rest of his life he remained on his estate at Petton. He married that same year, 1804, to a Miss Emma Walmesley. Their son, John Sparling, who became Rector of Eccleston, wrote a family history and described his father as a signal failure in dealing with all the grave interests of life; he was angry and irritable, and especially intolerant of children. Sparling lived on until 1870, having served as High Sherriff of Shropshire.

Samuel Renshaw remained as Rector of Liverpool until 1829, dying at Maghull. His daughter, Ann, never married, but lived at 5 Islington with three female servants. She died in 1856. The writer of the anonymous letter was never publicly identified.

The fatal duel at Knotts Hole was not the last to be fought in Liverpool. The next year, 1805, Major Brooks, a Customs Officer, perished in a duel which he had provoked with Colonel John Bolton, but that is another story.

Convicted by a Bandage

During World War Two, a brutal murder took place in the Waterloo area of Liverpool. The culprit was eventually brought to justice by an unusual clue which he had left behind at the scene of the crime.

It all began on the stormy evening of 2 November 1940, when fifteen-year-old Mary Hagan left her home in Waterloo to buy cigarettes and a newspaper for her father. When she failed to return from the errand, her father called the police.

The police organised search parties which combed the area and that same night, the body of the missing girl was discovered in a concrete blockhouse, which had been built to serve as an anti-invasion fortress. It was soon evident that the poor girl had been raped as well as murdered. As the detectives searched the ground around the blockhouse for clues, they came upon the distinct impression of a boot heel in the mud. Nearby, more clues were found: a piece of army bandage, stained with a zinc-based ointment that had obviously been used to treat a thumb wound, and a chocolate bar wrapper which also had small smears of zinc ointment on it. Forensic analysis revealed that Mary had eaten the chocolate bar. This meant that whoever had worn the bandage, had also come into contact with the murdered girl. If the wearer of the bandage could be found, then the police would have their killer.

There were thousands of soldiers stationed in Lancashire at the time, which left the police with the seemingly impossible task of tracing Mary's killer. However, they received a break when a young waitress came forward with a very valuable piece of information. She told detectives how a soldier with a cut on his face had asked her if he could clean himself up in her home. He claimed that he had been involved in a fight.

Then a series of other facts came together which linked the killing with a previous crime. A cyclist named Anne McVittie had been robbed by a soldier on a canal bank just a month earlier, less than a mile from the spot where Mary Hagan had been raped and killed, and the descriptions of the suspect wanted in connection with these crimes were very similar.

A fortnight after the waitress gave her description of the suspicious man, the prime suspect in the murder case, an Irish Guard from Seaforth, Sam Morgan, was arrested in connection with a robbery in London. An observant detective noticed how Private Morgan had a healed scar on his thumb. This information was wired to the Lancashire force, and a search of Morgan's Seaforth home commenced immediately.

A length of army bandage, which exactly matched the strip found at the murder scene, was retrieved from Morgan's house. Then more witnesses came forward to underline the soldier's guilt. The landlord of a public house told police how he had seen Morgan in his pub on the night of the murder, sporting a bloodstained cap. Furthermore, Morgan's boots perfectly matched the plaster cast that had been made from the footprint found next to the body.

Now certain that they had got their man, the detectives

arrested Morgan and led him away for questioning. He betrayed his guilt by his feeble smile and twitching facial muscles, as he lamely tried to insist that he had only robbed cigarettes and money from Mary, and had not brutally assaulted and killed her.

The evidence against Morgan was overwhelming and at his trial he was found guilty of the rape and murder of Mary Hagan. He was subsequently hanged on 4 April 1941, at Kirkdale Gaol.

The High Rip Gang

In 1874 a twenty-six-year-old doctor named Robert Morgan made an August Bank Holiday trip to New Ferry, accompanied by his wife and brother. Upon passing a public house in Tithebarn Street, a swaggering young ruffian named McCrave approached him and menacingly demanded 'ale money'. McCrave was a notorious member of the much-feared High Rip Gang, a large mob of violent criminals that held North Liverpool in a grip of terror.

Doctor Morgan was not used to being accosted in such a way and looked at the young delinquent with disdain. He then made the mistake of condescendingly suggesting that seventeen-year-old McCrave should work and not beg for his beer money. Upon this, McCrave's associates, two thickset teenagers, Campbell and Mullen, also aged seventeen, closed in on the naive physician. They knocked him to the ground with simultaneous punches, then cruelly kicked him along the street for a full forty feet. His screams for mercy went unheeded, and not a single member of the public came to his aid. His wife almost fainted at the sight of the vicious attack, and his brother was equally helpless, as other members of the High Rip turned up.

By the time the police arrived upon the scene, Doctor Morgan was already lying white and motionless on the pavement, dying from internal bleeding. It was too late to save him. In a state of shock, Morgan's brother finally snapped, and he suicidally chased after McCrave, and the murderous youth was captured in the brave pursuit when a policeman also gave chase.

Although McCrave remained tight-lipped about the identity of his accomplices, it was only a matter of days before Mullen and Campbell were identified and brought into custody. Mullen had been discovered trying to board a ship at the docks. The brutal death of the respectable Doctor Morgan at the hands of the High Rip Gang was reported across the land, and served to darken even further Liverpool's reputation as a rough and dangerous city. Even hardened criminals in Liverpool lived in fear of the High Rip.

In 1879, a tough docker named Georgie Yates of Anfield related to a reporter how he had lost an eye and suffered a broken jaw at the hands of two ferocious females who were members of the infamous gang. Both women had been barefooted and barely out of their teens, yet they behaved like prize fighters when they set upon Yates when he caught them robbing from a waterfront warehouse. Poverty was the mother of crime in the days of the High Rip, and, without in any way condoning such violence, it is plain to see that desperate people resorted to very desperate measures in order to survive.

McCrave, Campbell and Mullen were tried and sentenced to death for the murder of Dr Morgan. Their families sent a petition to the Home Secretary, begging him to let the boys off with a flogging, but it was rejected. However, at the eleventh hour, one gang member was saved. Campbell was reprieved and given a life sentence instead, because of good behaviour and a rather sudden, new-found devotion to the Bible!

The crime had horrified the British public, and justice had to be seen to be done, otherwise there undoubtedly would have been a riot. Most people were enraged at Campbell's reprieve, and there were many petitions asking for him to be flogged to death. However, the hanging of the ringleaders, McCrave and Mullen, did serve as a warning to the remaining members of the gang. When the day of execution came to McCrave and Mullen, the former was so petrified that he vomited and soiled his trousers as he was being led to the gallows at Kirkdale Gaol, on 3 January 1875.

The High Rip later disbanded and several less ferocious gangs falsely claimed to be splinters of the most evil mob ever to walk Liverpool's mean streets.

The Sad Fate of Louise Bencke

The infant mortality rate in Liverpool in the nineteenth century, as in so many other large cities at the time, was shockingly high. It was commonplace for families to lose several children within days of each other, when the frequent epidemics of diseases such as cholera and diptheria swept through the city. But did this situation make parents value their children less? The following story suggests that it possibly did.

In 1835 John Albert Bencke, a twenty-one-year-old man from Danzig, emigrated to Liverpool seeking employment. He soon secured a well-paid position in a timber exporting business at Liverpool Docks. Bencke was a clever, conscientious and hard-working individual, who eventually rose to realise his ambition of becoming the Consul for Wurtemburg, in 1858. After his retirement, he retained the title of Honorary Consul for the remainder of his life. In his late twenties he married a London woman named Elizabeth Hughes, and she bore him two children: Albert Henry, in 1846 and Louise Elizabeth, in 1851.

The fate of the latter child was discovered by the local historian extraordinaire, Jack Cooper, a man with an encyclopaedic knowledge of Liverpool.

Several years ago, Cooper came into the possession of John A Bencke's diary, and within its pages he uncovered a tragic tale which does not have a satisfactory conclusion. The diary was not kept on a daily basis by Bencke, but was written in hindsight and details his travels over the European continent. In one entry, Bencke records that baby Louise, aged sixteen months, was not well. He therefore decided to take his infant daughter and family away from the rainy, smoke-laden skies of Lancashire, and they embarked on a journey to Danzig, taking in a tour of the principal cities of Germany on the way.

Was Louise's failing health really the main incentive to embark on the trip, or was it the result of the characteristic restlessness of her father? We have no way of knowing. Sadly, the route which they took through Hamburg, Schwerin, Rostock, Berlin and Stettin, was an arduous one in those times, not at all suitable for such a young child, particularly one in a precarious state of health.

The baby's physical condition deteriorated throughout the journey and, on arrival at Danzig, poor little Louise Bencke died. Her tiny body was immersed in spirits of wine and was dispatched, unaccompanied, back to Liverpool, where she is said to have been buried in St James' Cemetery, off Hope Street. Her family continued on their travels, despite her death, visiting Leipzig, Wiesenfeld, Eisenach, Frankfurt and several other towns and cities, until they finally reached Waterloo. Only then did they decide to return to England.

The family's apparent callousness regarding the death of Louise, and her journey alone back to England, is difficult to explain. Perhaps the Benckes were in a state of shock, and continued the tour so that they could distance themselves from their tragic loss, at least temporarily.

The mystery surrounding Louise Bencke's final resting place is still unsolved. Jack Cooper has tried to locate her grave, but without success. The resting place of her father is a modest grave in St John's Cemetery, Knotty Ash.

If Louise, the privileged child of wealthy parents, met with callous unconcern, what hope was there for the thousands of urchins who inhabited the countless filthy courts and cellars of Victorian Liverpool? The following two contemporary accounts give some idea of the miserable lives which many of them led.

Stolen Childhood

In 1905, a book was published by Robert H Sherard, called *Child Slaves of Britain*, in which the author discloses the findings of an extensive survey investigating the welfare of children in all the major cities in England and Scotland. His findings did not make comfortable reading and revealed that, for thousands of children, life at the turn of the century was, at best, an unending struggle against cold and hunger. The edited extracts below give some idea of what life was like for the under-priviliged children in Liverpool.

'In the better parts of the town the stranger is not, as in so many other British towns, startled by ragged and appalling apparitions of child-life. Liverpool saves appearances in a manner essentially British. The children of the poor, who are driven onto the streets to trade, must present a respectable exterior. They have in Liverpool what they style the Liverpool Police-Aided Clothing Association; the police 'aid' by recommending cases to the charity. Liverpool does not want strangers to see the distress of its little ones. Respectability must be assumed at any cost. One might leave the city, after wandering the better quarters, under the pleasing delusion that here at least the children are protected.

It is the boast of the place that it was the first of all English towns to deal with the question of street trading. Indeed, in this respect, it certainly did lead the way, theoretically; the Liverpool Corporation Act of 1898 is a model of its kind. Under this Act, boys under the age of fourteen, and girls under the age of sixteen, who wish to trade on the street have to be licensed, and their conduct is subject to certain regulations, such as one which forbids them to enter public-houses to sell their wares. Excellent regulations, if the children only would, or could, observe them.

For the rest, it is fair to say that the other Corporations which have followed Liverpool's lead, and have studied the workings of the Act on the spot, describe it as most effective. Before Birmingham, for instance, passed its Corporation Bye-laws on the subject of street trading, Mr Aston was sent to Liverpool to study the system there. He spent three days and nights in Liverpool, reported enthusiastically and still speaks so. I pointed out to him that in three days there are many things that even a trained observer may overlook. As in Manchester, as in Birmingham, as in many other towns, where byelaws have been passed, the laws are passed by. Children trade without licences. Children misrepresent their ages to obtain licences. They disregard the limits of hours fixed for their observance and they ply their trades in public-houses, or anywhere else where they are likely to earn money. All the regulations in the world will not prevent them from disregarding the law when starvation and ill-treatment at home are the certain punishment which awaits them if they do not bring back a minimum of profit, which too often represents a maximum of effort.

Indeed, the Liverpool magistrates seem to understand the circumstances, and deal leniently with offenders against the

Corporation Act. Out of two hundred and sixty-five children who were brought up before the Liverpool Bench for trading without licences, two hundred and twenty-seven were purely and simply discharged and were, no doubt, hawking again the same evening, whilst in the neighbouring public houses, their parents toasted the magistrates with enthusiasm and the Corporation Acts with irony.

For one who knows Liverpool, the aspect of the comfortably-clad children of the gutter affords the saddest contemplation. Here respectability masks gaunt hunger and life amidst surroundings the most dreadful. Liverpool, in the matter of its slums, plays with its cards on the table. It has not the hypocrisy of London or of Glasgow. You can find districts in Liverpool where you may walk for hours through streets of pestilence and death. Liverpool displays its sores. It packs its poor into awful cantonments, and it is, for instance, in that dreadful district of which Limekiln Lane is the main thoroughfare, that you can peep behind the mask of the children's respectability, police aided.

This most dismal slough is the habitation of casual labourers, of sailors, of the unhappy men who do odd jobs at the docks. In very many of these homes it is the miserable earnings of the children that are for weeks together the only income of the family. Here it is not parental greed that is to blame for the enslavement of the little ones; it is what is so radically wrong in the social conditions of the town. So overcrowded is the city of Liverpool and so fallacious are the hopes of employment that its docks hold out to the thousands who pour into its slums from the country, that the casual labourer who can get one full day's work in a week of days may deem himself one of the elect of fortune. I have seen men who have beaten the town and the docks for six weeks and who have only earned one day's wages. But for the puny efforts of the children, there would not enter these cottages a single scrap of food. Indeed, what money is earned either by the mother with a hawker's basket, or by the children in the various employments which are open to them, usually suffices not more than to pay the rent and to help the miserable families to play at hide-and-seek with starvation.

Tea – that is to say tea-leaves - stewed over and over again, and bread, are the staple articles of diet in these regions, and very often there is no bread to go with the tea. The days when a halfpennyworth of soup can be fetched from the soup-kitchen of the Food and Betterment Association, are red letter days in the squalid annals of these unfortunates. Under these circumstances, it will be easy to understand that the children must work. The average rate of pay which a boy or girl can earn in Liverpool is slightly over a penny an hour, and given that a lad can put in forty-eight hours out of school-time, the rent for that week is at least assured.

Where the children are too young to go on the streets, the difficulties of the mother are enhanced. She must go out with her basket and the children must be left at home. One hears of deserted babies being roasted slowly to death in domestic accidents during the forced absence of their mothers.

A staple industry with the children of Liverpool is that of knocker-up. So many men have to be down at the docks at early hours in the morning, that it is necessary for them to be roused. That big men may not oversleep, little children must undersleep. On bitter, dark, winter mornings you may see little shivering wraiths flitting from house to house, beating a tattoo on the murky window-panes, until a volley of oaths betokens that the task is done. I believe that a knocker-up with a good connection can earn from eighteen pence to half-a-crown a week, and by the time his rounds are over, the hour has come for him to begin the delivery of milk.

The curing of fish is another local industry which gives much employment to children. In filthy rooms, haddock and codling are smoked into table delicacies. The room is full of evil-smelling smoke, and from the pallet on the floor, on which the smaller children are lying, the noise of continuous coughing accompanies the greasy sizzling of the fuel. There is a little money to be got at this trade, but it has its drawbacks, and you can tell a child who is a curer of fish, by the chronic inflammation of his eyes. I know of two lads who, in this way, keep a home over their mother's head.

The home is one room in a three and sixpenny cottage. The woman's husband is at sea most of the time and his wages are very small. The woman's only resources, apart from the labour of her children, are obtained by borrowing on the security of her absent husband's wages from one of the women-usurers of Liverpool. The rate is one penny on every shilling for one week, and if you fetch the shilling on Friday evening, the interest is due all the same on Saturday morning. It is of course inconvenient, the woman being an invalid with lung-trouble, that the smoking of the fish should be carried out in the one room where she lies coughing, but these are things which cannot be helped.'

Chemical Nightmare

Another chronicler of the lives of the poor and their children, this time in Victorian England, was Robert Blatchford. On his travels, he visited the town of St Helens in Lancashire, not far from Liverpool, with a view to finding out more about the working conditions within the chemical industry, and he wrote about his experiences in his book, *Dismal England*, which was published in 1899.

'If, leaving Liverpool, you visit the neighbouring towns of Widnes and St Helens, you will be struck by the beauty and the healthy appearance of the children. Of the children, I say, in contradistinction to the 'young persons'. When, at thirteen or fourteen a child becomes a young person and may be sent to the chemical works as a full-timer, the gradual devastation of Nature's beautiful temple begins. In quite young people you can already note the inroads that the poisonous gases of the stills are beginning to make.

On the teeth, first of all, then on the eyes, and then on the lungs, the devilish influence of the lethal air exerts itself. I do not know which spectacle is more chilling to the heart: the man, still in the prime of life, who, three parts killed in the chemical works, is being finished off in the workhouse, half-blind, toothless, choking with asthma and groaning with chronic kidney disease, or the young person, upon whose face and body the dreadful stigmata of the trade have already been imprinted, vouchers for the fulfilment of his certain and terrible destiny.'

However, despite his intention to do so and his usual thoroughness, Blatchford did not actually visit the chemical works in person. The reason for this departure from his normal practice is explained in his book:

'Now, why did I come away without going into those chemical works? There were several reasons – I was told that pressmen were not welcome there, but I might have gone without a welcome, it was pouring with rain, but in spite of the influenza bacillus I might have braved a wetting. The reason for my discretion will be found in the following dialogue between a chemical worker and Mr King, the President of the Chemical and Copper Workers' Union:

"He might run through, just for a glimpse. One of you could lend him a coat."

"Yes, we could lend him a coat; but we don't want him gassed."

"But if he covered his mouth up?"

"Oh yes. He might manage it; only, if he wants to get away to-night and if he should happen to get a whiff of gas."

"To be sure. But you can take precautions. Take some whisky in with you."

"We'll do our best; but we cannot guarantee safety. You know the risk, and none of us is safe ourselves."

At which point I felt curious enough to ask a few questions, and thereon ensued another dialogue, as follows, this time between the chemical worker and myself:

"What do you mean by 'getting gassed'?"

"Inhaling the chlorine gas."

"Does it hurt?"

"Feels like swallowing boiling water with quicklime in it."

"Is it dangerous?"

"Sometimes."

"What does it do to you?"

"Knocks you down."

"What do you take for it?"

"Whisky."

"How long are you bad?"

"A few hours, or a few days."

"Is there much risk?"

"There's a big risk, and if you are not used to it, nor aware of it. You might get burnt with the lime, or the caustic. And the heat's very trying to strangers, and many objects to the stink."

"Have you ever been gassed?"

"Many's the time I've been gassed with gas that blew over from another works five hundred yards off. The men get gassed through their flannel masks. The gas has been known to knock down a horse in the open air."

"I think I will go round the works some other day, when I have more time. I am in a hurry this evening."

The reader can draw his own conclusions. I wanted to see these men at work; but I could not afford three days in a St Helens hospital, and I don't think boiling water and quicklime would be a nice drink.

What I want to convey to you is an idea of the conditions under which the men work in the chemical trade at St Helens. As to the men, the work is too laborious, the work is very dangerous and unhealthy and the hours are long. The wages are too low and the moral and physical conditions are abominable.

St Helens is a sordid, ugly town. The sky is a low-hanging roof of smeary smoke and the atmosphere is a blend of railway tunnel, hospital ward, gasworks and open sewer. The 'features' of the place are chimneys, furnaces, steam jets, smoke-clouds and coalmines. The products are pills, coals, glass, chemicals, cripples, millionaires and paupers. The population is estimated at nearly eighty thousand, most of whom are engaged in the staple industries of mining, smelting, glass-blowing, shopkeeping, stench-making, slave-driving and slow murder.

The chemical men work amid foul odours and in intense heat – the temperature being often as high as one hundred and twenty degrees. They sweat and toil in an atmosphere charged with biting acids, or deadly gases, or dense with particles of lime. They have to stand at the scorching portals of the furnaces, manipulating ponderous masses of blazing matter, or to lift heavy weights, or to wheel burning salt in iron trucks and barrows, or to plunge into lethal chambers piled with blistering ash and thick with stifling vapour, or to manage huge cauldrons of scalding caustic.

Flying particles of caustic sting them like wasps and the lime and acids sear and gash their skins and rot the teeth in their gums. Deadly gases and pungent dust rack and wear out their lungs, and often spread them out in helpless agony on the floor. Their shirts rot to tatters on their back and the clogs burn off their feet in a few days' time. They are obliged to drink to excess, and that of ardent spirits, to keep themselves at work. They undergo immense physical strain and suffer such severe bodily pain, that they are old men at forty. Their hours vary from seventy-two to eighty-four hours a week, and their wages from three shillings to eight shillings a day.

We will begin with the powder-packing, which consists of a series of desperate rushes into a chamber where the floor is fire and the air is death, for the purpose of shovelling bleaching powder into casks. The packer has his head tied up in a kind of pudding bag, his eyes covered with hideous goggles, and the lower part of his face swathed in from twenty to forty thicknesses of flannel. Through this flannel he inhales the air, which, being thinner than the gas, can penetrate. His nostrils are left free, and through them he exhales the air. Let him take one sniff up through his nose, and he is gassed. It takes a long time to learn to breathe in this way, and even when learned ...

... even then. I saw a man rigged up in an ordinary room where there was no gas. He was a horrible sight. He looked half-strangled. His face, or what was visible of it, was swollen black-red; his nose was livid. His eyes seemed to bulge up under the hideous spectacles, yet he has only been dressed in that way for five minutes. But fancy our brother in the powder chamber for an hour in the heat and the gas!

I turn from him to a man who works in the lime sheds. He works in an atmosphere of floating lime particles. He is muzzled, like the powder-packer, and breathes in the same way. His flesh is greased all over. Twenty minutes in the lime shed is enough at one time. Then he must go out to rest and breathe. No man could endure more. These men dare not wash themselves. Sometimes they are not washed for months, except in grease. They work for seventy-two hours a week, and earn as much as thirty-three shillings a week. The lime scorches their flesh. They cannot rest in bed sometimes. In the summer it is worse. All these poor creatures dread the summer.'

The investigations of Robert H Sherard and Robert Blatchford show us how wickedness comes in many forms, many of which were perfectly legal. Appalling working conditions, for both children and adults, which could lead to serious injury or even death, coupled with meagre wages which could barely sustain them, were the norm in the nineteenth century and the early part of the twentieth.

Workers who sustain serious accidents in the workplace in modern times are quick to receive medical attention from first-aiders and an efficient ambulance service, but the labourers of nineteenth century Liverpool endured a stomach-churning variety of horrific deaths and injuries in the workplace, simply because sensible safety measures had not been established. Cost-cutting firms cut short a lot of workers' lives.

Accidents Will Happen

On 11 May 1835, a faulty safety valve, which governed the pressure in a boiler, failed on the premises of Messrs Ring and Vickess, a sugar boiling plant on Ford Street, off Vauxhall Road. The cylindrical copper boiler became so distorted by rapid expansion, caused by the tremendous pressure of steam and bubbling caramel trying to escape. It became alarmingly puffed up into a spherical shape. The factory workers, seeing what was happening, fled for their lives, and one woman even dived headfirst through an open window.

The boiler exploded with horrific results. The blast completely decapitated one worker, but at least his death was swift. Molten caramel and searing steam blasted at the other workers as they were thrown across the room. The evacuated factory workers in the street shuddered, as they listened helplessly to the terrible screams. The wife of one of the men ran inside and fainted at the sight which met her eyes. Her husband's face had been burnt to such an extent that it was skeletal, and two blackened smoking sockets existed where his eyes had been. In a state of extreme shock, the man felt around his blistering face and his fingers poked about inside the empty eye sockets. He let out an agonised scream, then keeled over and died. The other two had died instantly from blast injuries. The proprietor of the plant was not held responsible in any way and no compensation was offered to the victims' families.

In a cruel twist of fate, John Candles, the brother of one of the dead men who perished in the Ring and Vickess plant, met his own death in an appalling accident ten months later, on 1 March 1836, when the house he was living in on Thomas Street suddenly collapsed. Candles and five other people were crushed to death, and nine more were seriously hurt. The house's dilapidated foundations were blamed for the collapse. John Candles had suffered a particularly agonising death, because he had been sitting in front of the blazing coal fire before the house fell in on him, and within moments, he was pinned down, immersed in the glowing coals.

***

Shortly after the Thomas Street tragedy, in April 1836, a gruesome freak accident blighted the matrimonial plans of Miss Nelly Radcliffe, a pretty sixteen-year-old bride-to-be. Nelly was described as having the countenance of an angel, with large blue eyes, a button nose and cupid's bow lips, all set upon a cherubic face that was crowned with a head of golden curls. She lived with her parents and six brothers at a shambling, overcrowded house on Upper-Pownall Street in south Liverpool, and was looking forward to her marriage in two days' time.

Nelly was engaged to Edward Steele, a fish porter from Great Charlotte Street. As Nelly left her home on an errand for her father, a sudden fierce gust blew a loose slate off a neighbour's roof. The slate hurtled down and embedded its sharp edge in Nelly's face. It split the girl's face length-wise, from the forehead, down the bridge of her nose, through the nose cartilage, to the upper lip. Nelly collapsed and fainted. She was found shortly afterwards by a chimney sweep, lying in a pool of blood.

Cosmetic surgery was in its infancy in those days, and a surgeon simply used coarse sutures to stitch up the long horrific gash disfiguring what had been a lovely face. The resulting scar was deep and livid red, and ran in a jagged red line from Nelly's forehead down to her mouth, almost bisecting her nose. The wedding was cancelled and Edward Steele coldly broke off his engagement to the facially-scarred teenager.

Nelly Radcliffe never got over the accident, or her rejection by her fiancé, and she hanged herself from a banister at her home one year later, after leaving a suicide note and a sealed envelope. The note tried to explain her reasons for committing suicide to those she left behind. 'Children avoid me in the street and people stare,' read a part of the sad note. The sealed envelope which Nelly left was addressed to Edward Steele, but he apparently tore the missive up without ever reading it.

Buried Alive

Premature burial was once a relatively common, terrifying prospect. In the 1960s, an ancient graveyard in what was then West Germany was demolished to make way for a car park, and a third of the corpses ploughed up by the bulldozer showed disturbing signs of having struggled whilst in their coffins. The most grisly evidence included skeletal fingers broken by frantic scratching at the immovable coffin lid, and tell-tale fracture lines on the frontal parts of skulls where the buried person had smashed his or her head against the coffin lid in a desperate, but ultimately vain, attempt to escape the unimaginable silent and asphyxiating blackness of the grave.

Here in Liverpool, I am in no doubt that people have been buried alive, usually by accident, but even, sometimes, on purpose. In volume one of *Haunted Liverpool*, I related the well-documented account of a certain Thomas Cregeen Williams, a businessman of Leeds Street, whose intact body was discovered in a sheet iron tube off Great Homer Street in 1945.

His corpse was fully clothed in the typical Victorian attire of the period, and several diaries covering dates from June 1884 to July 1885 were found in his jacket. There were no injuries to the body, nor any signs of a struggle, so Mr Williams either voluntarily crawled into the cylindrical tomb, was unconscious, drugged, or perhaps even drunk before he was pushed inside, or, he was simply threatened and forced possibly at knifepoint. He was not poisoned, because a forensic pathologist tested the cadaver for any such substances, and none was present.

A lid was subsequently fastened onto the end of the cylinder, creating an airtight seal, so we must assume that Mr Williams died from slow asphyxiation, as the small amount of air in the metal coffin ran out. Who was the person or persons responsible for the death of Mr Williams? To this day, no one knows. What is known is that Williams was having serious financial problems with his paint and varnish factory at 18-20 Leeds Street and, perhaps to escape the strong-arm tactics of creditors eager to recoup money owed to them, Williams intended to be smuggled out of his factory in what would appear to be a cask of paint or varnish. If this was the case, then perhaps he accidentally suffocated and maybe his accomplices panicked when they realised that he had died. We may find out more about the man in the iron tube one day, if enough research is carried out.

In January 1868, a team of Liverpool workmen were drafted in to dig up two thousand bodies from St Peter's graveyard in Church Street. All the bodies were removed with the utmost decency and propriety, and were re-interred in Anfield Cemetery. Some of the coffins dated as far back as 1707. However, during the careful excavations, it was found that many coffins – many of which dated back to 1707 – had rotted to such an extent that they fell apart as they were hauled out the ground, spilling out their human remains.

One body, draped in a white silk shroud, fell out of such a crumbling coffin into the mud. Two workmen picked it up and were about to place it on a stretcher, when they noticed the bent back fingernails attached to the skeletal fingers, and a dark extensive stain of what had been blood on the shoulder. The jaws of the skeleton were biting into the stained area, the teeth still intact. The workmen had seen such evidence of premature burial before. The buried person had awakened in his grave, and had broken his fingernails as he clawed at the lid of the coffin in a frenzy of unimaginable fear. As the effects of choking asphyxiation and madness took their toll, the desperate, doomed man had actually bitten into his own flesh.

The superstitious often mistook the bloodied shrouds of exhumed corpses as evidence of vampirism, but the truth was just as terrifying. It is probable that such vampire reports were simply cases of people who were unlucky enough to come out of some cataleptic state that an inept doctor had mistaken for death. This would explain one such account reported in 1548.

That year, Liverpool was almost depopulated when two hundred and fifty men, women and children died from a highly contagious plague. The bodies were thrown into a lime pit on the outskirts of the town. A girl (age not given) who was believed to be dead from the plague, emerged from the pile of bodies. She staggered out of the mass grave at night, and the superstitious people of the day fled from her, not only because the girl was probably a carrier of plague, but also because she was thought to be in league with the devil to rise from among the corpses. Stones and other missiles were hurled at the unfortunate girl, and she was driven out into the countryside, where she probably perished of starvation, shunned by everyone.

Eyeball to Eyeball

The time was precisely 3.30am on a freezing January morning in 1899, when a common thief crept up the black-iced back alleys of Renshaw Street. The street was deserted, except for a solitary caped policeman on his lonely beat along the deadly quiet thoroughfare. As the sentinel stars shone down on that crystal-clear moonless night, the 'bobby' continued past the old Adelphi Hotel and turned up Copperas Hill, unaware that the sharp eyes of a consummately clever thief were watching his every step.

Silent as a ghost, the nocturnal criminal, fifty-six-year-old Henry Swann of Moon Street, surveyed the immediate area once again, before closing in on the pillar box. Swann produced a leaden weight smeared with bird-lime from an old metal cigar tube. Attached to the weight was a five foot length of fishing line. The modus operandi of Mr Swann was to fish for letters in the pillar box with the sticky weight. He had had some sizeable returns from his 'angling' as he called it. Even today, people often send money through the post, and in the days of Henry Swann, it was a common occurrence to send banknotes, coins, jewellery and other valuable items through the efficient and trusted postal system.

Swann tugged the line, and sensed he had a catch. He reeled it up and manipulated the padded envelope through the mouth of the pillar box. Three more letters were extracted before Swann decided to quit while he was ahead. He had pushed his luck on the previous night and had almost been seen by a lamplighter, so he quickly shut down his nefarious operation. He thought he heard a voice and froze like a startled rodent, but was soon relieved when he realised that it was the snoring of some noisy sleeper in Heathfield Street who had left his window slightly ajar. Soon the policeman would be round again on his clockwork patrol, so Swann deposited the gummy weight in the cigar container and wound the twine around its cylinder. Up Leece Street he moved stealthily homewards, with the four envelopes tucked snugly against his belly under his belted coat.

Moon Street once ran from Crown Street, until, like the many old streets of Edge Hill, it was levelled in the 1960s to make way for the sprawling campus of Liverpool University. At a dingy terraced house on Moon Street in 1899, Henry Swann lived with his nine-year-old nephew, Edwin Quinby, who was an orphan.

Upon that frigid January morning, Mr Swann entered his home, bolted the door and checked that the curtains were drawn. He lit a candle from the flickering flames in the grate, then positioned it on the table. With relish, he laid the envelopes out ready for inspection. Swann was just in the middle of poking the sealed flap of the first one with an old oyster knife, when the door of the parlour steadily opened. Swann's heart almost stopped with fright. It was young Edwin, unable to sleep because of the relentless, permeating arctic cold.

"I'm freezin' uncle," Edwin sniffled and walked eagerly to the remains of the coal fire with a fuzzy woollen blanket cocooned around him.

"I'll knock your 'ead off next time you barge in like that,"

Swann warned the boy, then resumed his lucky dip with the envelopes.

The first one contained a three-page letter composed in illegible, spidery handwriting. It was tossed into the fire, and Edwin gleefully rubbed his hands as he watched the letter curl and shrivel in the flames.

The second envelope was opened. Again there was nothing of any value, only a love letter of florid prose and feverish ramblings penned and signed by a 'Mr X' and addressed to a Miss Elizabeth Paine of 75 Bedford Street. This missive was also delivered into the grate. Edwin, who loved fire, picked up the flaming envelope and letter with a pair of tongs and watched it burn away to carbon flakes.

The third envelope contained a skilfully-executed begging letter, written by a man whom Swann knew well – William Cooke of Sandon Street. Cooke, a failed alcoholic solicitor, had syndicates of begging letter writers, who used his 'templates', as he called them, to extract substantial sums of money from the soft-hearted and the plain gullible. The letters, signed by various names and bearing different return addresses, were targeted at people on a list of known philanthropists. This was one begging letter which would surely go unanswered. Swann crumpled the sham epistle into a ball and hurled it accurately into the fire.

The fourth envelope – a rather padded one at that – was opened. Henry Swann prayed for some return from his fishing trip. It was a piece of muslin cloth. He pulled it out of the envelope and unwrapped what looked at first like a scarf, but it was soon apparent that it was not. The material swathed a letter – and something so awful that it caused Swann to recoil loudly in terror and disgust. In his hand sat a pair of human eyes!

Edwin dropped the tongs with fright as his uncle yelped and recoiled from the grisly package. Swann hurled himself backwards from the table, scraping the rickety-legged chair across the bare stone floor with a screech.

"What's the matter uncle?" enquired the trembling lad, as he rose from the fireside chair.

Swann was speechless. His eyes were transfixed by the lifeless staring blue irises on the table. Those slimy white disks were actually someone's eyes. They had belonged to a real person who was now blind or dead, Swann reasoned, as he broke out in a clammy sweat.

Edwin edged cautiously towards the table, trying to determine what the strange circular convex white disks were.

"Stay put! Stay there!" Swann bawled, and his nephew obeyed.

"What are they uncle?"

"Eyes," Swann replied, gripping the back of the chair, "they're eyes."

The repulsive objects of fear were the sliced-off frontal sections of human eyeballs, but who had cut them off? A murderer most likely, Swann conjectured. He had to go to the police to tell them about the appalling discovery; but he would have to pretend that he found the envelope on the pavement on Renshaw Street. If the police did not believe him, he would be in real trouble. Also, how could he explain the smears of bird-lime on the envelope? Worse still, Swann pondered on the possibility of being implicated in a possible murder. He regretted fishing at the pillar box in Renshaw Street. Why had he not he tried the pillar box on Brownlow Hill? Because he had seen a policeman on point duty earlier that night; that was the reason, Swann recalled.

"Whose eyes are they?" Edwin asked, hiding in his blanket as he stood behind his confused uncle.

"I don't know," Swann admitted.

He leaned forward and quickly snatched the leaf of notepaper that had been mailed with the hideous staring eyes. His hand shook with a nervous tremor as Henry Swann whispered out the words of the note:

'Dear Mr Appleyard,
I enclose a pair of eyes taken from your daughter's suitor. The rest of him shall follow soon.
Yours faithfully,
a madman who is watching your home.'

The disturbing communication confirmed Swann's darkest suspicions; that he had unwittingly embroiled himself in a murder, and a particularly nasty one at that. Perhaps if he simply burned the letter and the eyes, it would be the end of the grave entanglement, but would that not be a crime? Destroying evidence of a murder? Swann had to do something fast before dawn. He considered sending Edwin to the police with the murderer's letter! But Edwin was a dullard who spoke after he thought, he was sure to slip up and probably even tell the police all about his pillar box fishing expeditions.

Swann anxiously paced back and forth, repeatedly colliding with his nephew, who was following him like a young chick. He suddenly halted and lapsed into a brown study as he looked into the flames. He pictured himself passing the police station, dropping the accursed letter on the pavement under the blue lamp before scuttling on into the night. He quickly dismissed the idea. The very thought of walking in close proximity to a police station, carrying human eyes in an envelope, gave him butterflies in his stomach.

Then an idea surfaced from his subconscious. Fighting back fear and nausea, he carefully scooped the rubbery eye cross-sections up with the end of the killer's letter, then placed the notepaper and the sliced organs on the muslin cloth. He wrapped the muslin cloth around the letter and the eyes and, with a shudder, shoved the bundle back into the envelope. He sealed the flap with wax from the candle, then turned to Edwin and stooped so that he was at eye level with the boy.

"Listen carefully. Take this letter, and go straight to the pillar box in Abercromby Square. Post it, and come straight back. If you see a bobby, and he doesn't see you, come back home. If a bobby stops you and asks you what you've got, tell him that a stranger gave the envelope to you. Have you got all that?"

Edwin nodded doubtfully, and beheld the envelope with a look of horror.

At 4.30am, Edwin Quinby embarked on the short journey from Moon Street to Abercromby Square. Flecks of snow whirled down as the ink-black starry skies clouded over, and Edwin squinted as he paced quickly down Bedford Street through the biting north wind. The streets gradually took on a ghostly appearance as the powdery, wind-driven snow dusted their buildings, lending a spectral aspect to the architecture.

As Edwin was crossing Chestnut Street, he heard a voice. Through the wrought iron railings of a house he caught a fleeting glimpse of a bearded, scruffily-dressed man who was sitting on the steps leading down to a basement door. Edwin panicked. He started to lose his footing as he tried to run over the snow-covered cobbles of the road. The man, who seemed to be a vagrant, shouted something unintelligible and gave chase. Edwin slipped during the chase near the corner of Abercromby Square and grazed his kneecap. The beginnings of a blizzard commenced as the man towered over the fallen boy.

"Give me that!" he growled menacingly and reached for the parcel.

Edwin backed away slightly. A glimmering light caught his attention further up Oxford Street. It was the bull's eye lantern of an approaching policeman.

"A bobby's coming!" Edwin shouted in an optimistic tone, and pointed at the constable, who was now blowing his whistle.

The vagrant twisted round, eyed the policeman, then ran off up Bedford Street. The officer of the law gave chase for a while but soon gave up and ran back towards Edwin.

"What are you doing out on the streets at this unearthly hour?" he asked Edwin, who began to mumble and stutter.

The wax seal on the envelope had broken when he fell, and the policeman picked up the envelope and examined it suspiciously.

That morning at 5.15am, detectives and policemen hammered on the door of Henry Swann's home in Moon Street. Mr Swann knew that he should not have trusted Edwin with such a straight forward, yet important, task, and he cursed the boy as he ran into the back kitchen. Two more policemen hammered on the backyard door. It was no use. Swann opened the front door and he was instantly apprehended.

The house was searched as two detectives questioned him about the letter. Swann immediately confessed to the pillar box theft but denied any involvement in the murder. A policeman soon discovered the cigar tube and the leaden weight coated with quicklime. Swann's house was searched from top to bottom, and the police then took him to the bridewell off Dale Street, where he was interrogated. By noon, Swann was released, and, due to his co-operation in helping to solve a more serious crime, received nothing more than a remarkably generous caution for the serious offence of theft from the Royal Mail pillar boxes.

Swann enquired if the police had managed to discover the identity of the murderer who had sent the repulsive eyes to Mr Appleyard. And, although he was under no obligation to do so, the detective decided to explain the background of the sinister letter.

Since November 1898, James W Appleyard, a music teacher of Catherine Street, had been receiving a stream of poison pen letters, as well as a variety of shocking items delivered by post to his home, including a dead rat, faeces, and other vile and disturbing items. Two of the letters bore Chester franking marks, but the rest had been posted in central Liverpool. Through a strange twist of fate, Mr Swann had unknowingly provided the police with a possible clue to the identity of the lunatic posting the letters and parcels to Mr Appleyard, when the letter containing the eyes had been intercepted in Renshaw Street.

A detective on the case had long held a theory that the man posting the distressing items had been a medical student who had briefly dated Mr Appleyard's daughter, Clara, the previous year. The student in question was discovered to be an opium addict, and so Mr Appleyard forced his daughter to break off her romance with him. Some time later, Clara became engaged to a shipping clerk.

Not long afterwards, the hate mail began to arrive. The spiteful medical student was lodging at the Rotunda Buildings, Rotunda Place, off Bold Street, within a short distance of the pillar box where the eyes had been posted to Mr Appleyard. The eyes contained traces of the kinds of spirits used to preserve medical specimens, and despite the letter's claims, the eyes of Clara's suitor were still intact. Her fiancé – Mr Blackwood – was in the best of health in Edinburgh, where he was conducting business.

However, concrete evidence which would prove that the medical student was behind the campaign of postal terror was still lacking, so detectives paid the trainee surgeon a visit. The young man was evidently surprised and apprehensive when detectives quizzed him and searched his digs. Although no evidence was forthcoming, Mr Appleyard never again received any obnoxious letters or parcels – and Henry Swann never went fishing in pillar boxes again.

Other titles from Bluecoat Press

If you have enjoyed the stories in **Wicked Liverpool**, you might wish to read more of Tom Slemen's work. The following titles, published by The Bluecoat Press, are available:

Haunted Liverpool 1 £5.99
Haunted Liverpool 2 £5.99
Haunted Liverpool 3 £5.99
Haunted Liverpool 4 £5.99
Haunted Liverpool 5 £5.99

Bluecoat Press have also published these true crime books:

The Cameo Murders by Barry Shortall £6.99
A gripping account of the famous Liverpool case. Shortall challenges the reader to read the book and then try and answer the question: Would you find George Kelly and Charles Connolly guilty beyond reasonable doubt?

Lady Poisoners by David Parry £8.99
David Parry, in these dark and disturbing accounts, has provided an insight into the warped and twisted minds of some of the most infamous women in English criminal history.

The Murder of Julia Wallace by James Murphy £8.99
The Wallace Case is unique: it is the only *not proven* murder case in English legal history. An unsolved, perfect murder, it is the 'nonpareil of all murder mysteries'. Murphy's perspective on the case is fresh, also looking at who Julia Wallace actually was.

Hard Cell by Frank Cook and Matthew Wilkinson £5.99
Hard Cell is about life in our prison system: the routine violence, drug culture, rapes and murder. The descriptions of inmate life have rarely been portrayed in such vivid detail. The book is about the ultimate failure of the prison system, which spends £25,000 a year keeping a prisoner in custody, in an environment which reinforces criminality and removes self-esteem and hope.